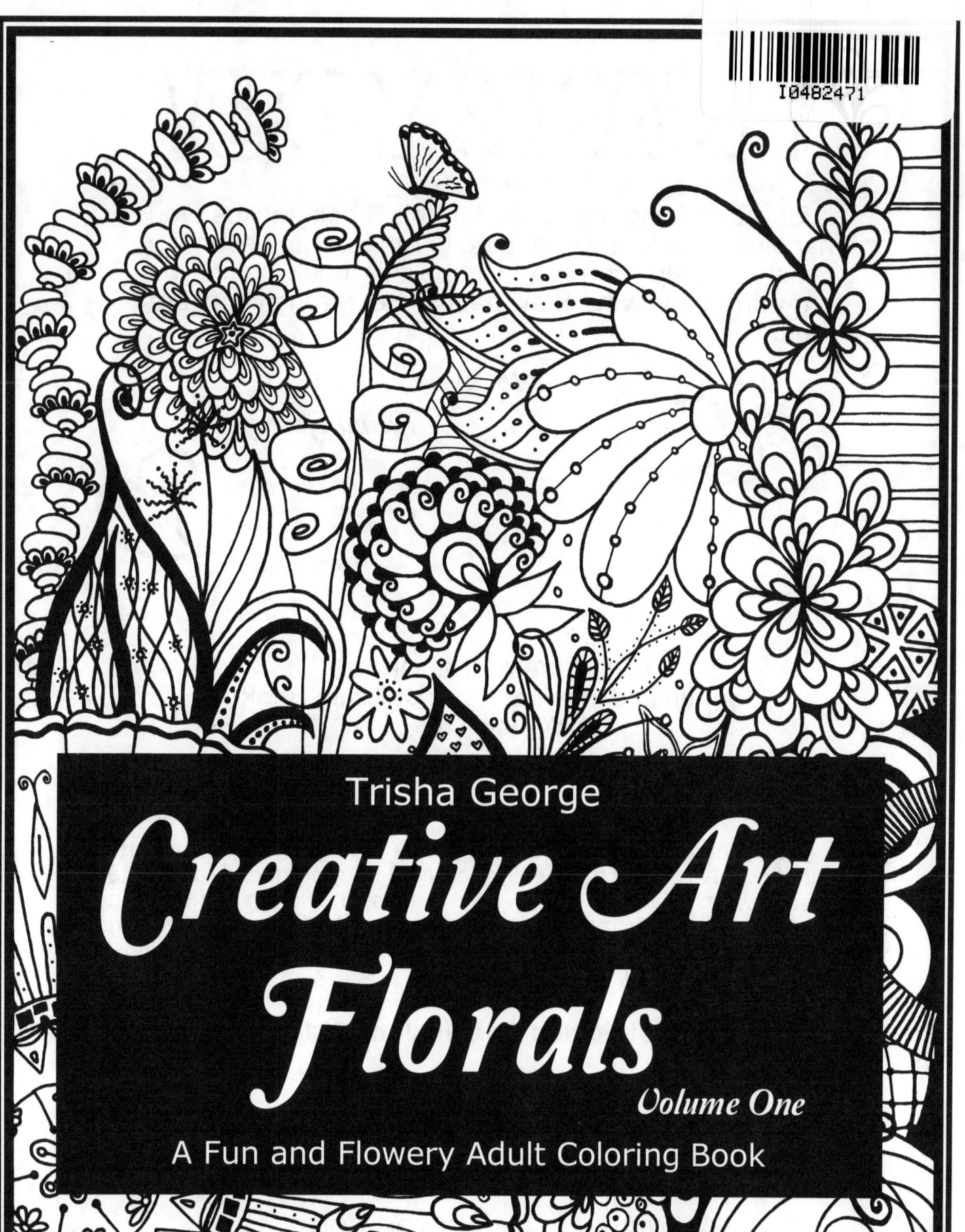

Trisha George

Creative Art Florals

Volume One

A Fun and Flowery Adult Coloring Book

THANK YOU!

...for purchasing my book. If this book makes you happy, I'd like to ask you to go to Amazon and submit a review to help me grow. I hope this book helps you grow in some way. Stay happy. Be Strong. You are beautiful!

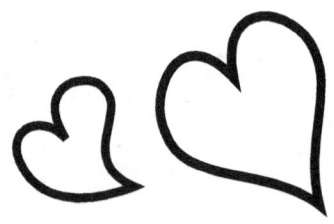

with love,
Trisha George

CREATIVE ART FLORALS
A Fun and Flowery Adult Coloring Book
Volume One

Copyright 2016 by Trisha George
All rights reserved.

First Edition Printed June 2016

ISBN-13: 978-1533353191
ISBN-10: 1533353190

For more information, please visit:

www.TrishaGeorge.com

THIS BOOK
BELONGS TO:

_____

Colored By: _____

Date: _____

Techniques/Media Used: _____

_____

_____

Please use pencil to fill in information.

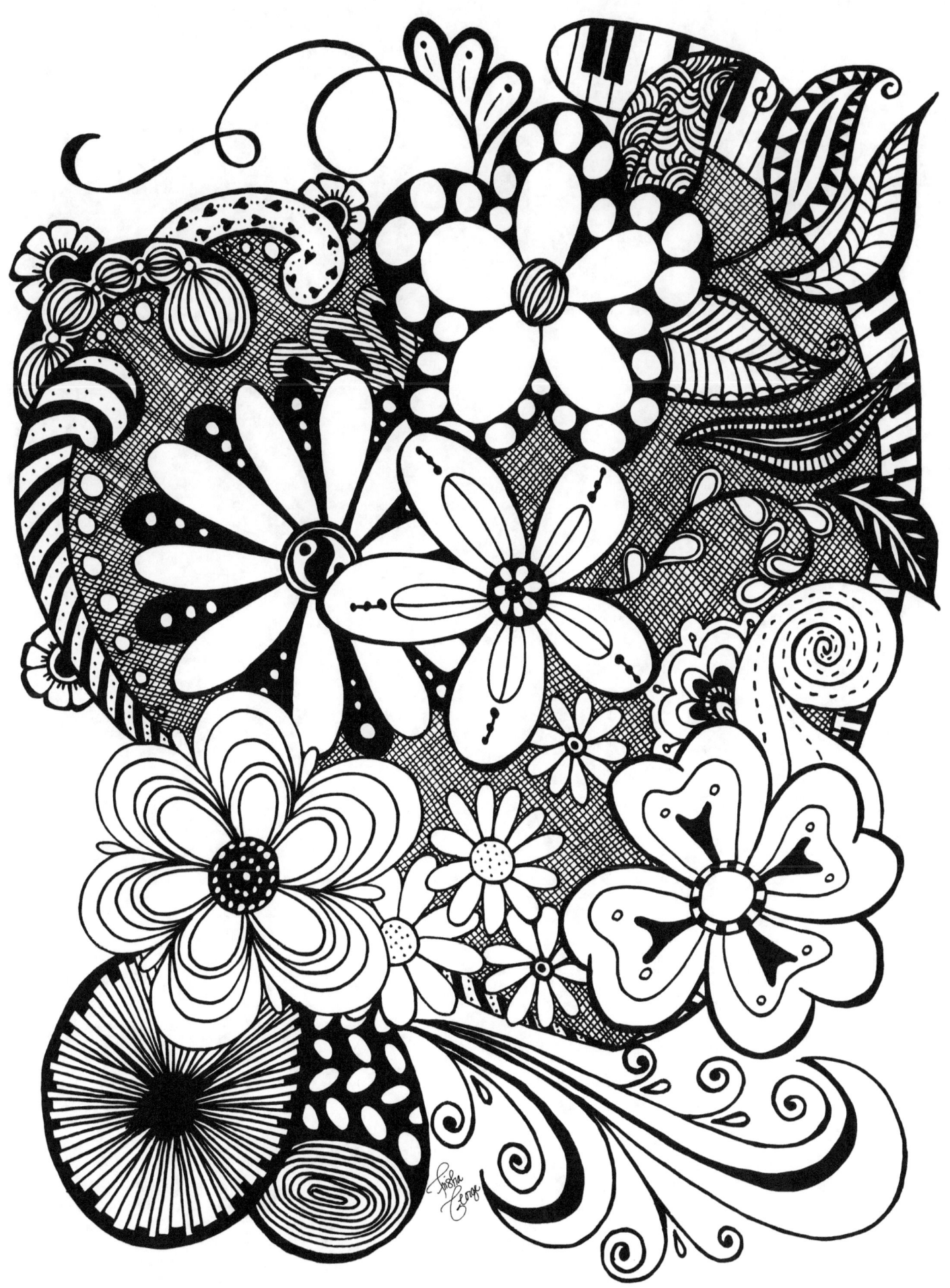

Colored By:_____

Date:_____

Techniques/Media Used:_____

_____

_____

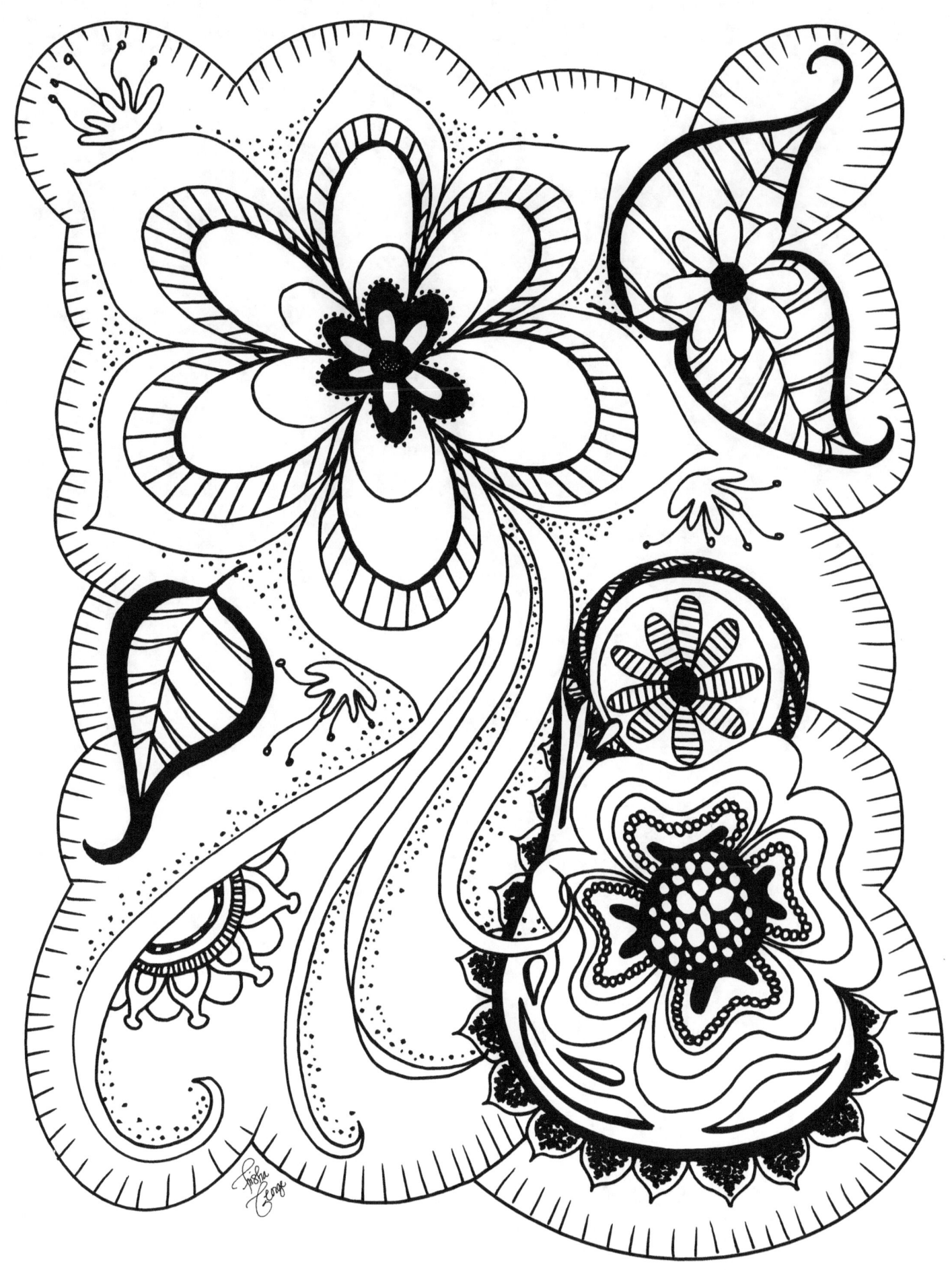

Colored By: _____

Date: _____

Techniques/Media Used: _____

_____

_____

Please use pencil to fill in information.

Colored By:_____

Date:_____

Techniques/Media Used:_____

_____

_____

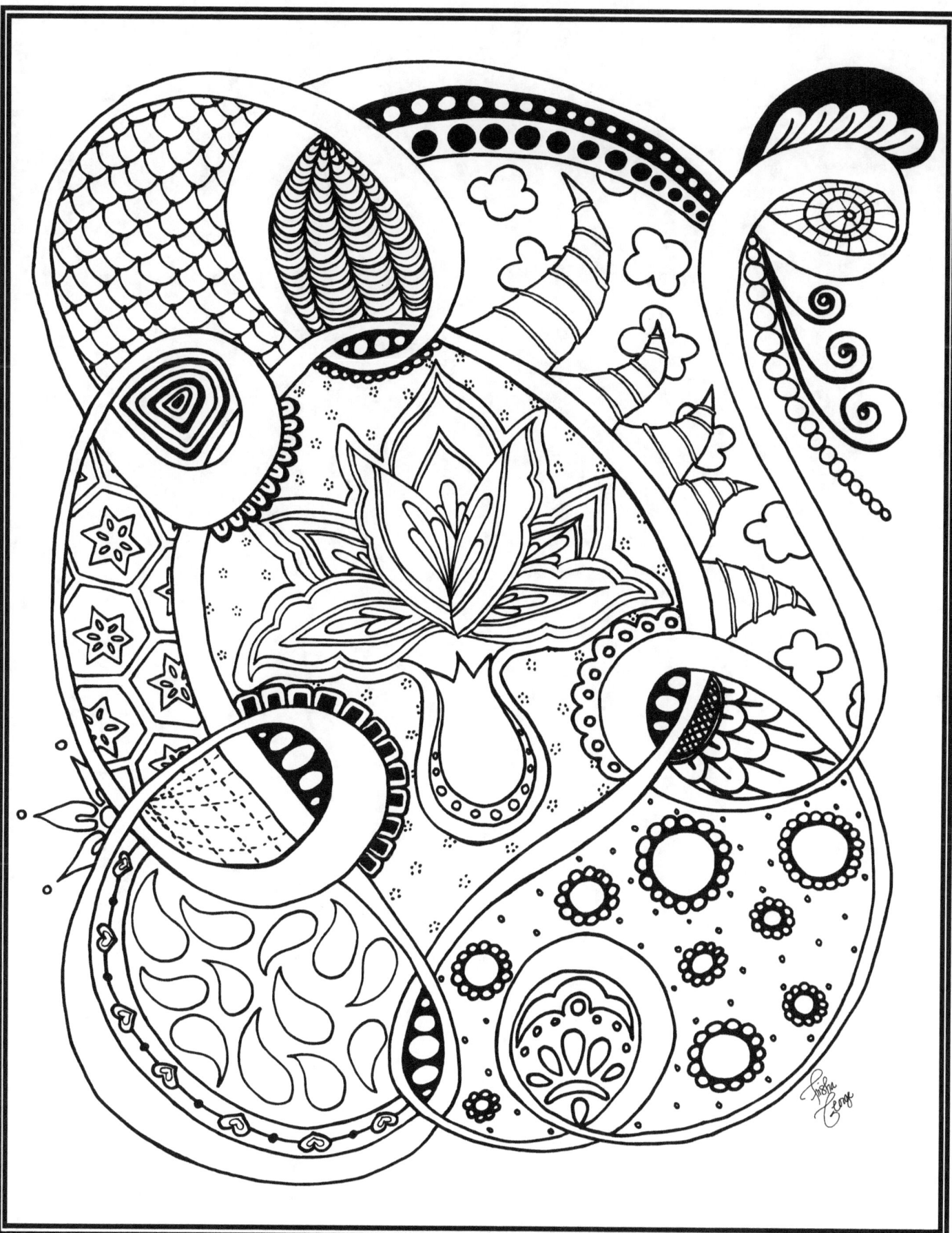

Colored By: _____

Date: _____

Techniques/Media Used: _____

_____

_____

Please use pencil to fill in information.

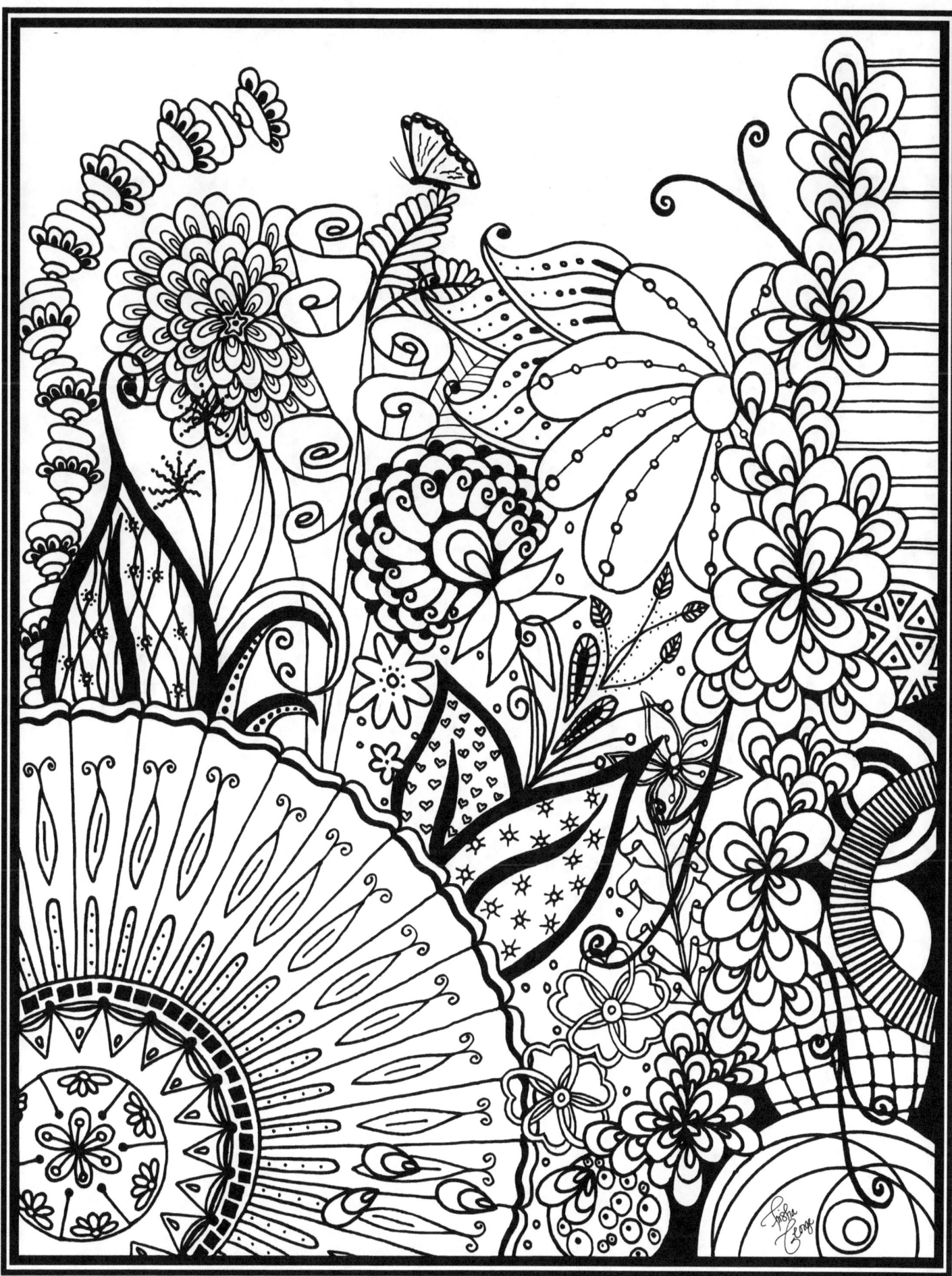

Colored By:_____

Date:_____

Techniques/Media Used:_____

_____

_____

Please use pencil to fill in information.

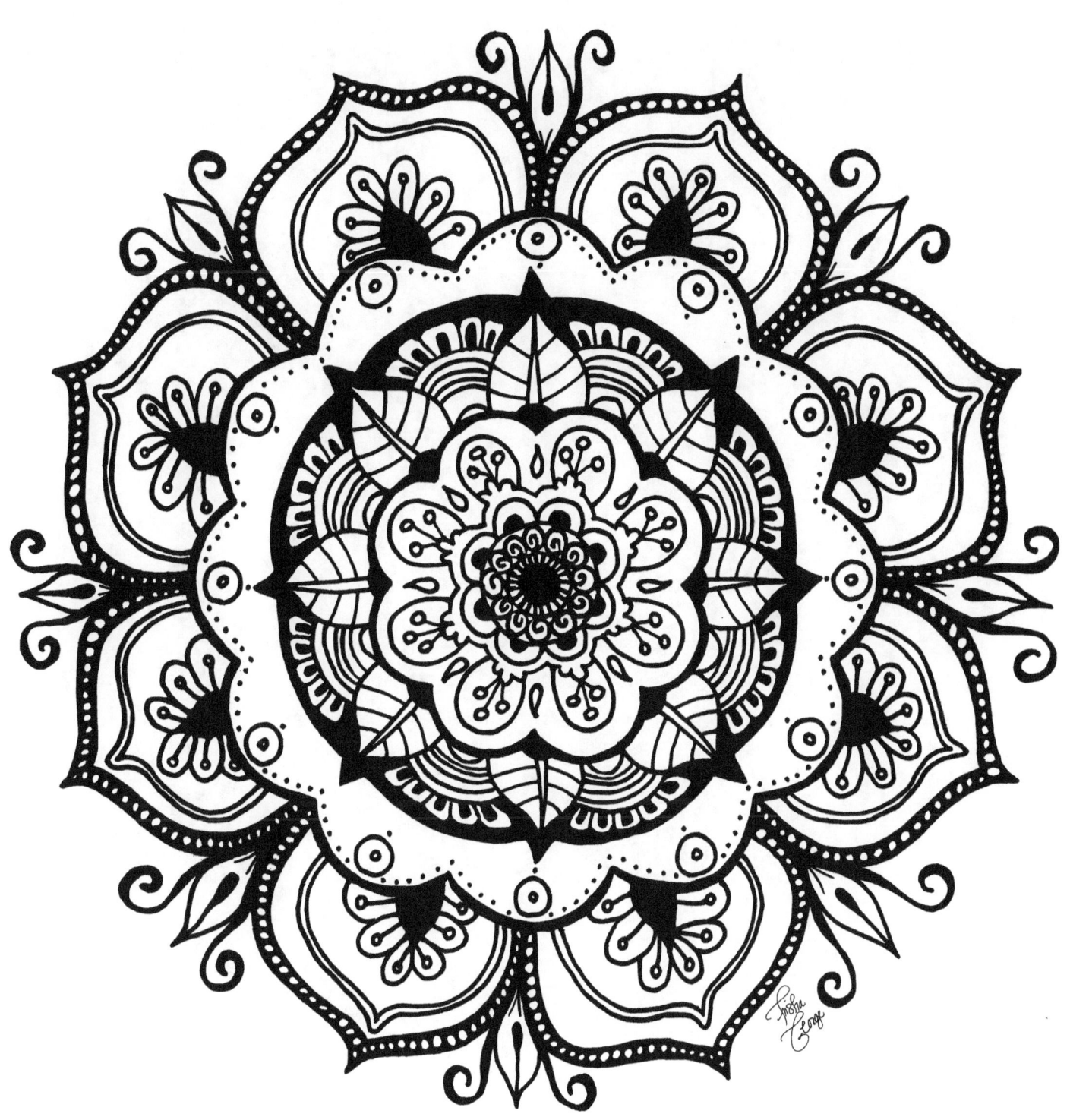

Colored By:_____

Date:_____

Techniques/Media Used:_____

_____

_____

Please use pencil to fill in information.

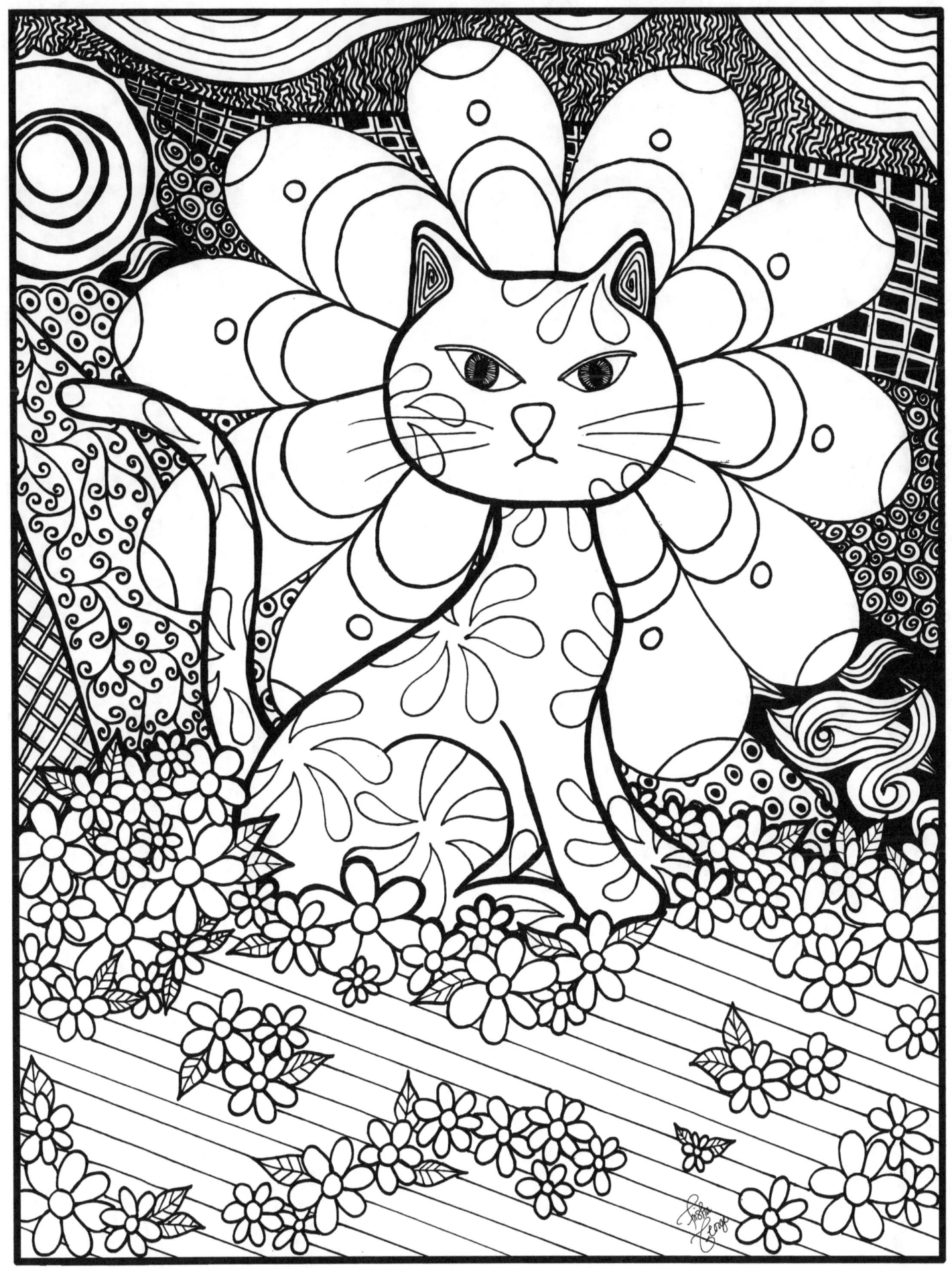

Colored By: _____

Date: _____

Techniques/Media Used: _____

_____

_____

Please use pencil to fill in information.

Colored By:_____

Date:_____

Techniques/Media Used:_____

_____

_____

Please use pencil to fill in information.

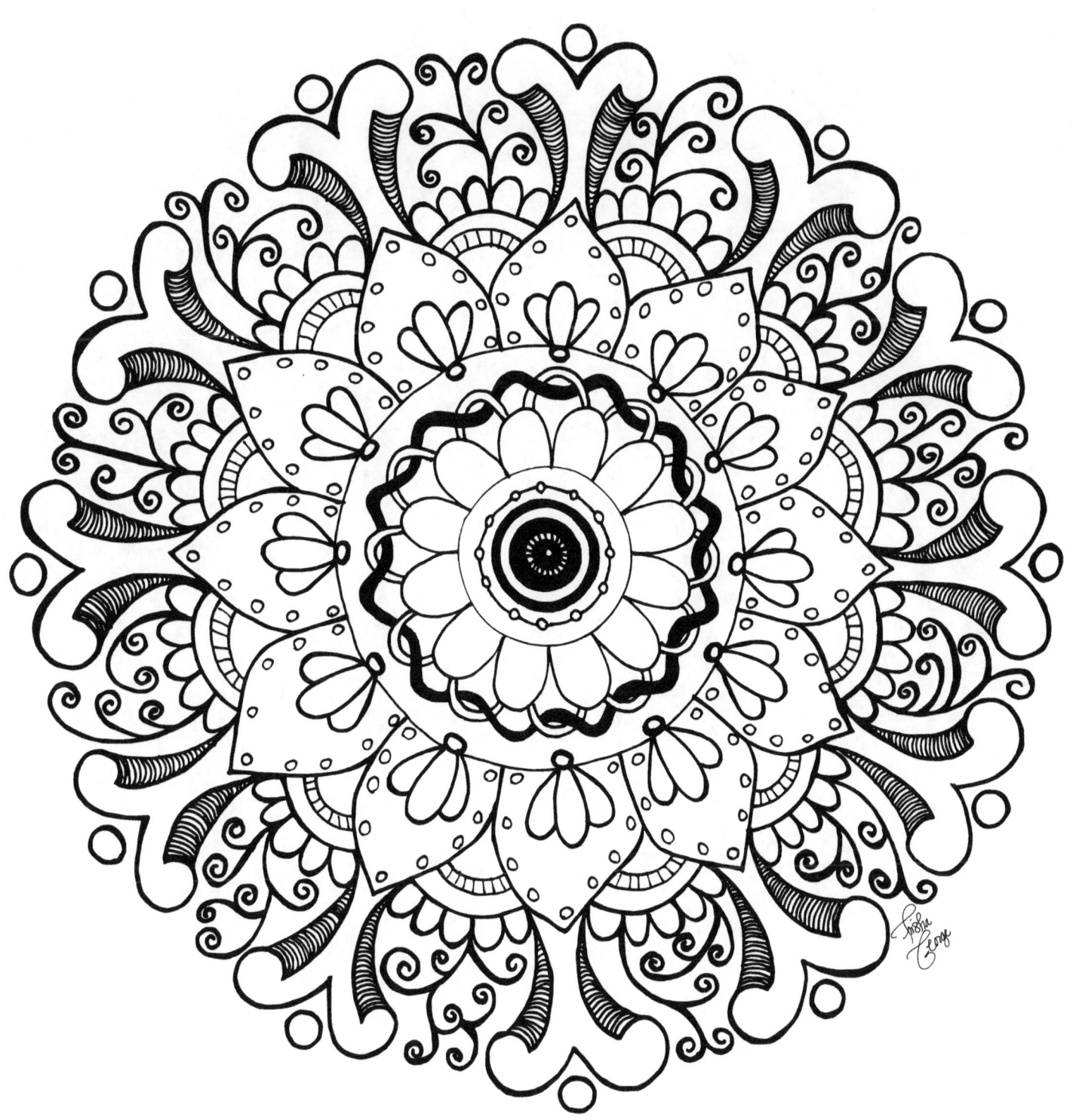

Colored By: _____

Date: _____

Techniques/Media Used: _____

_____

_____

Colored By:_____

Date:_____

Techniques/Media Used:_____

_____

_____

Please use pencil to fill in information.

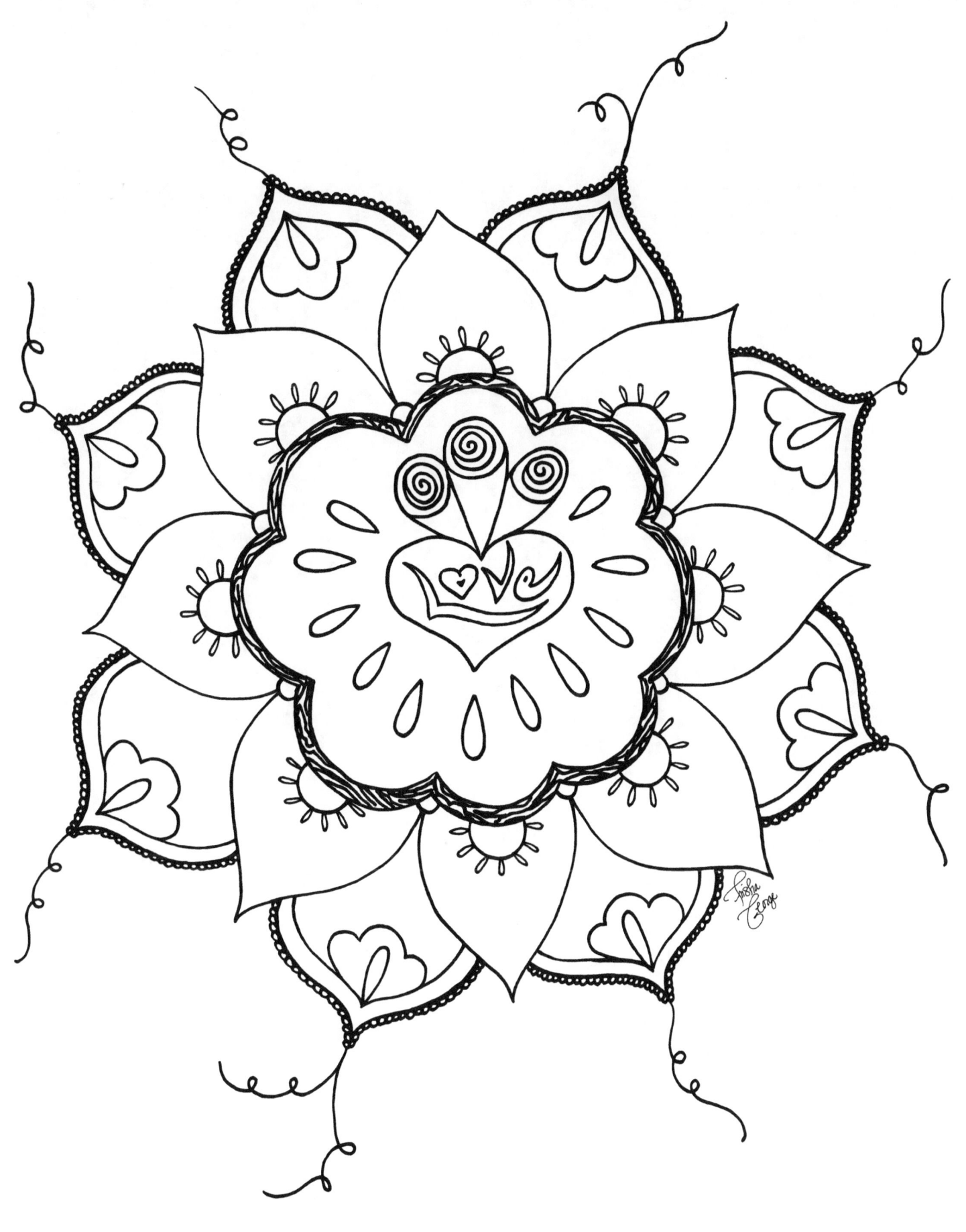

Colored By: _____

Date: _____

Techniques/Media Used: _____

_____

_____

Please use pencil to fill in information.

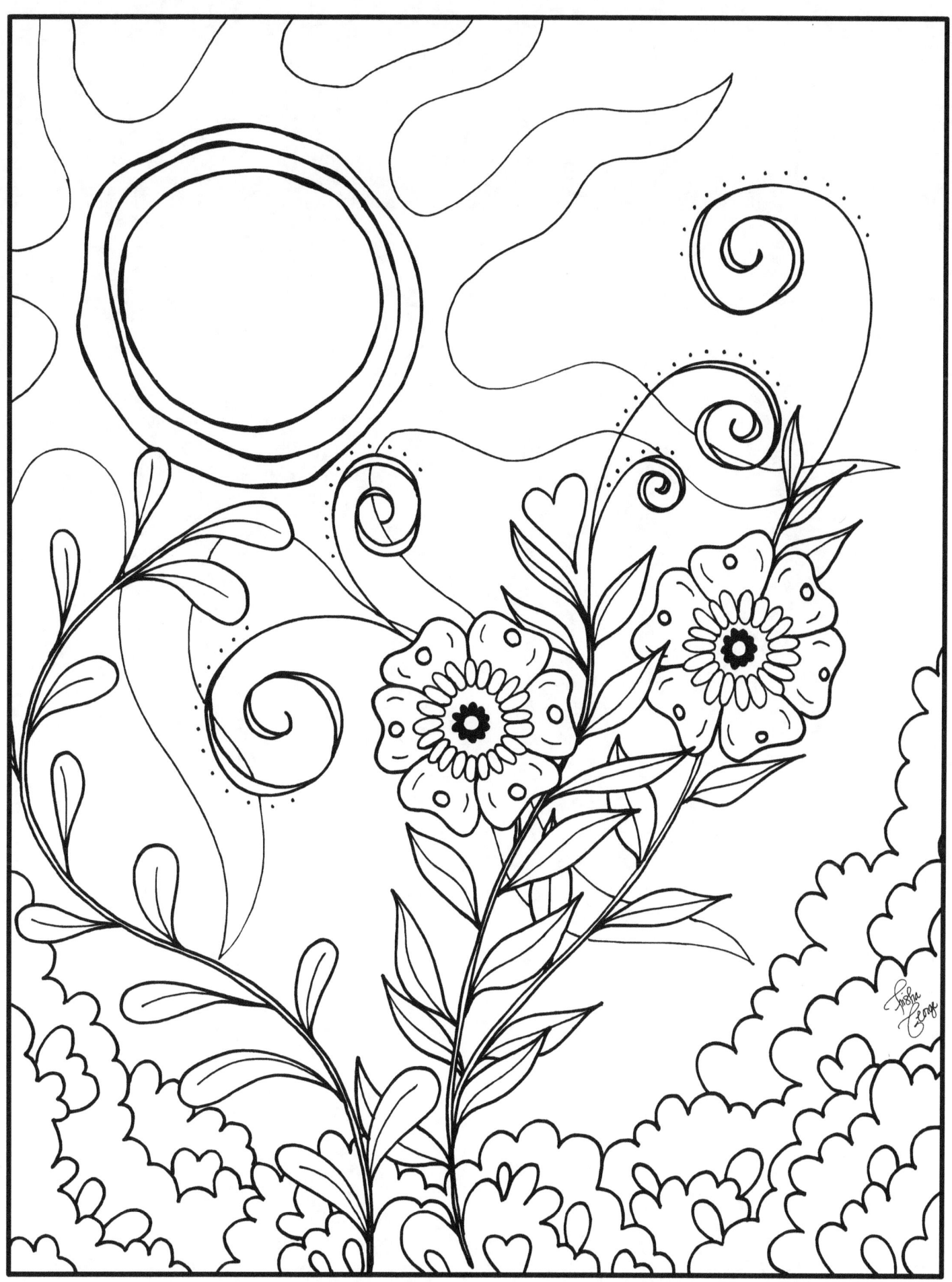

Colored By:_____

Date:_____

Techniques/Media Used:_____

_____

_____

Please use pencil to fill in information.

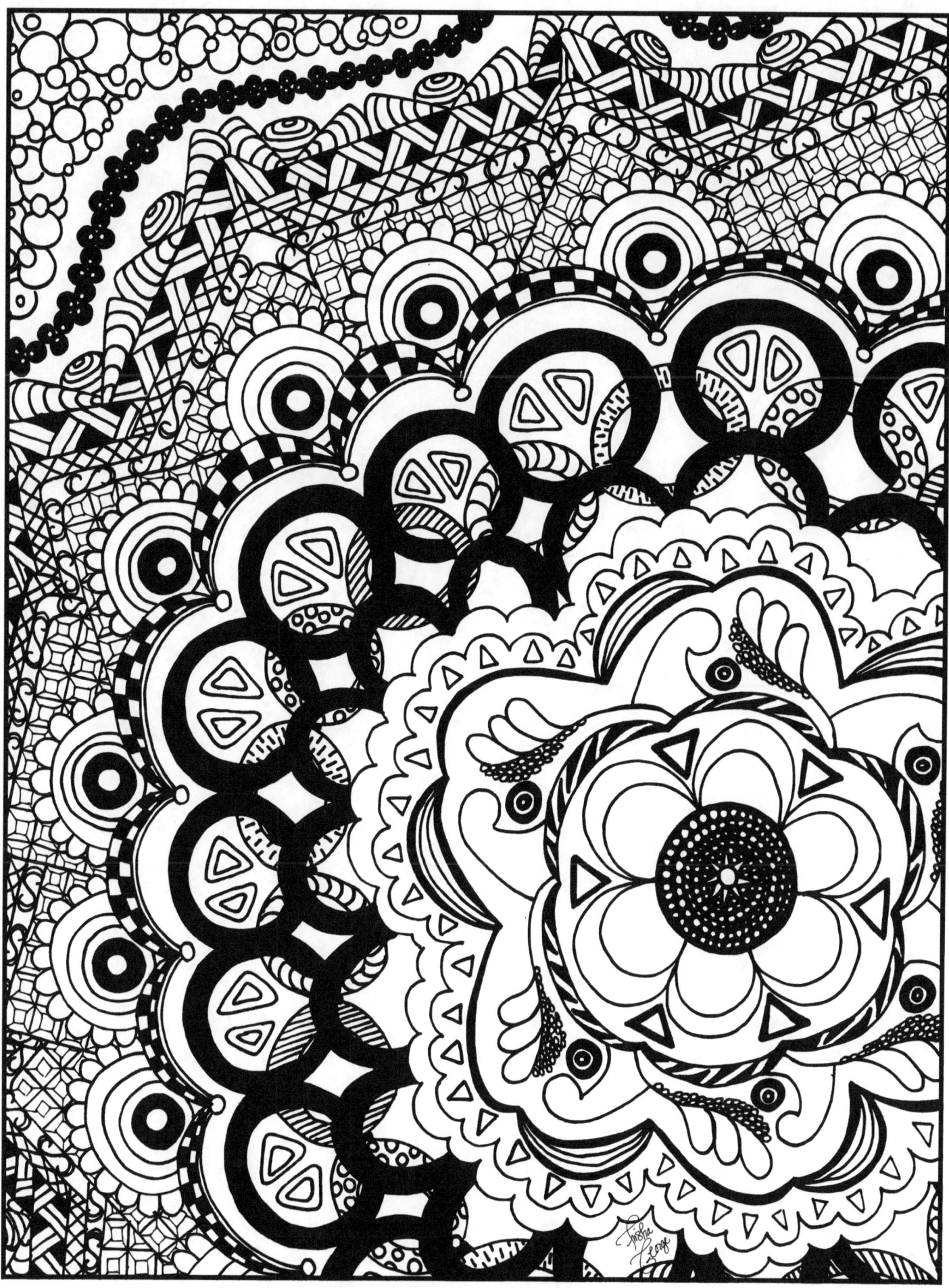

Colored By:_____

Date:_____

Techniques/Media Used:_____

_____

_____

Please use pencil to fill in information.

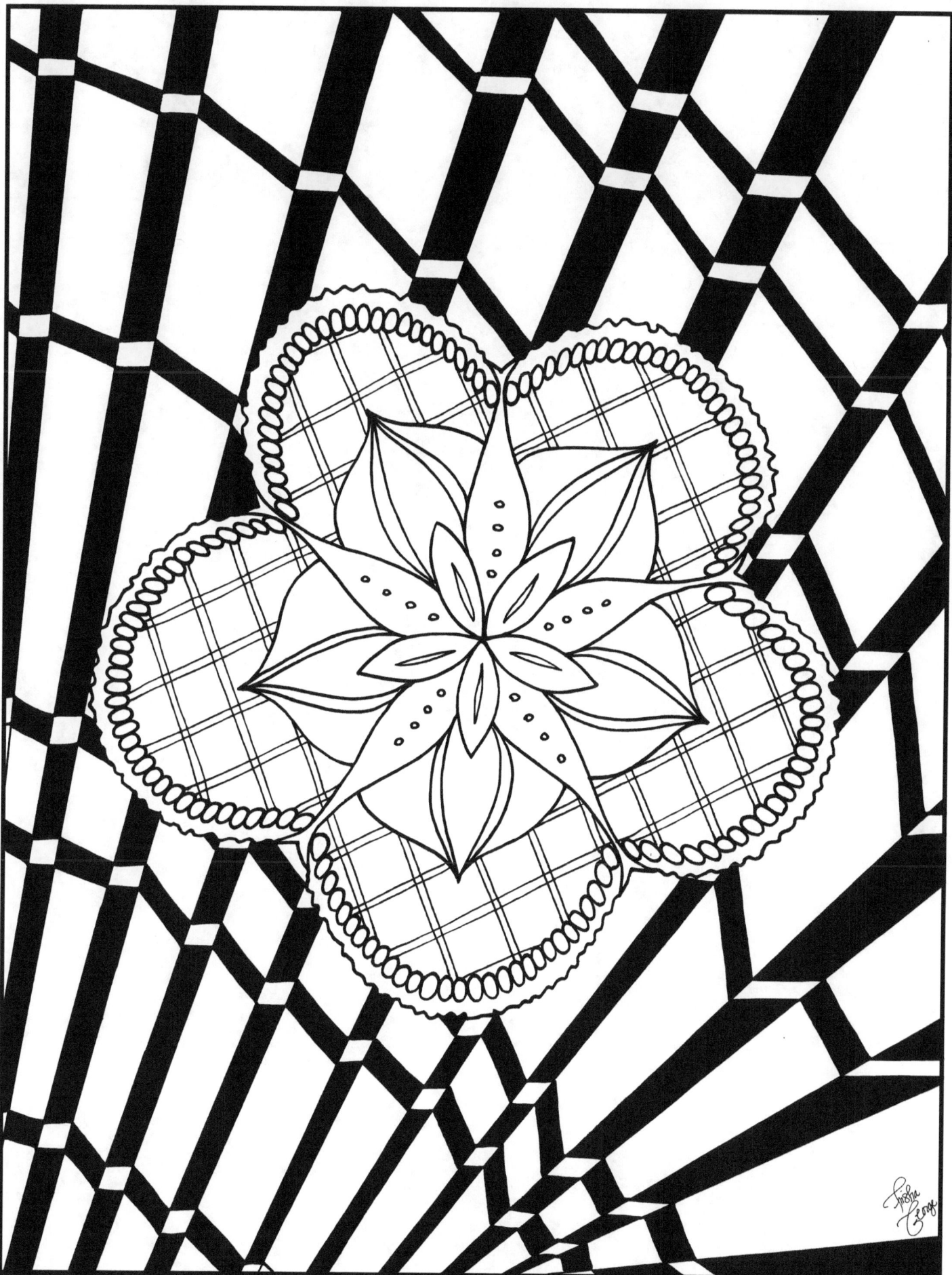

Colored By:_____

Date:_____

Techniques/Media Used:_____

_____

_____

Please use pencil to fill in information.

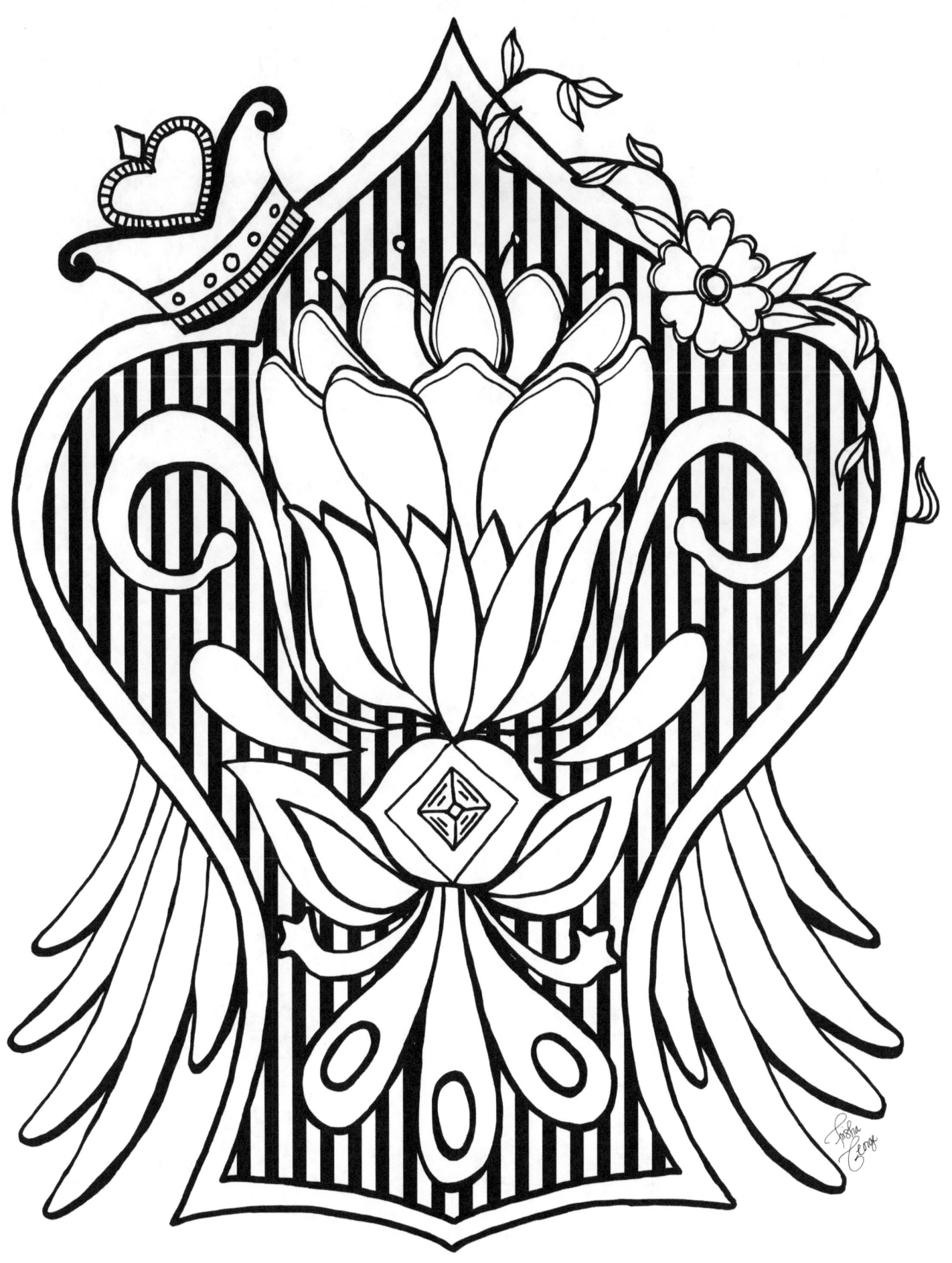

Colored By:_____

Date:_____

Techniques/Media Used:_____

_____

_____

Please use pencil to fill in information.

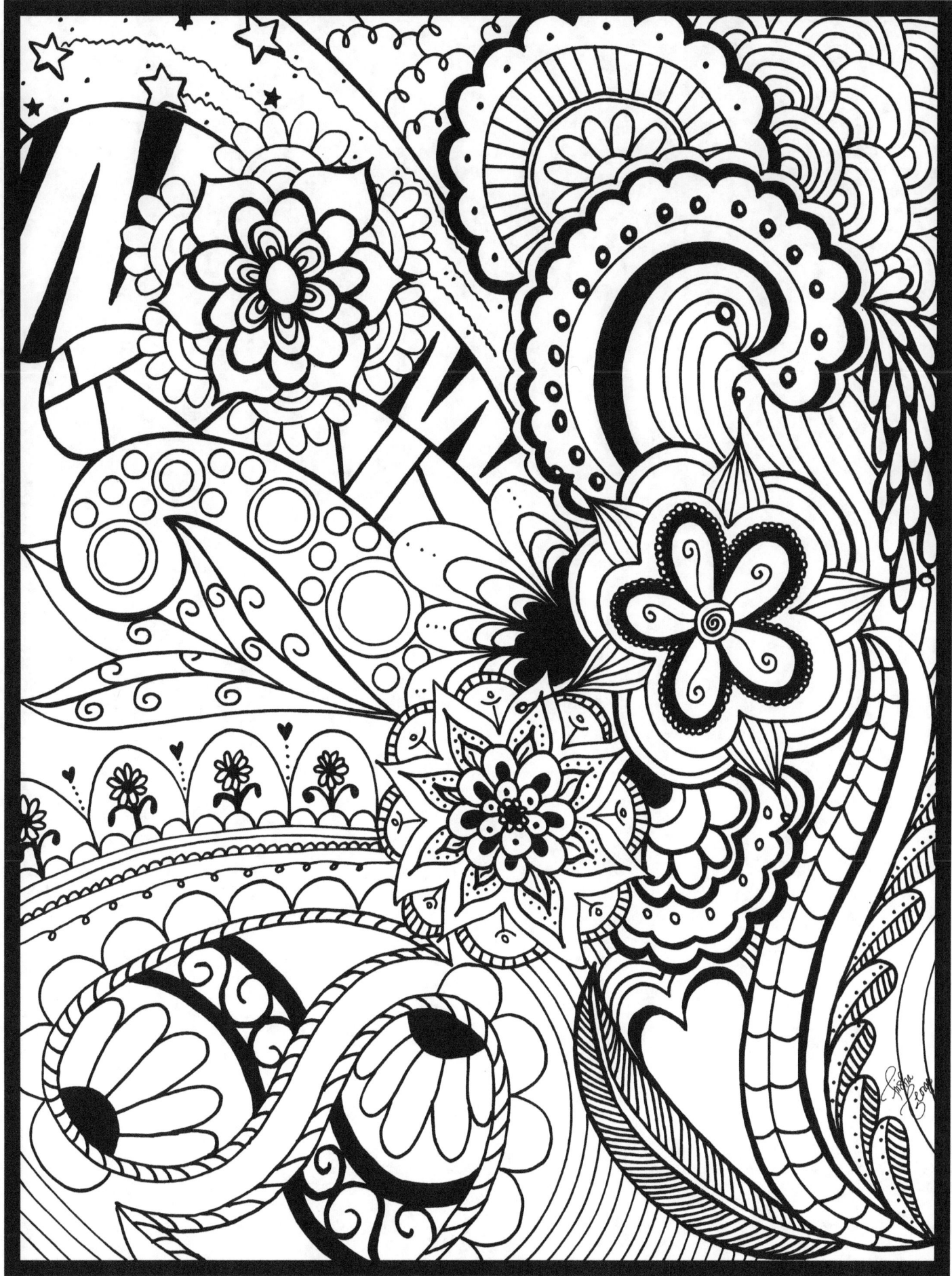

Colored By: _____

Date: _____

Techniques/Media Used: _____

_____

_____

Please use pencil to fill in information.

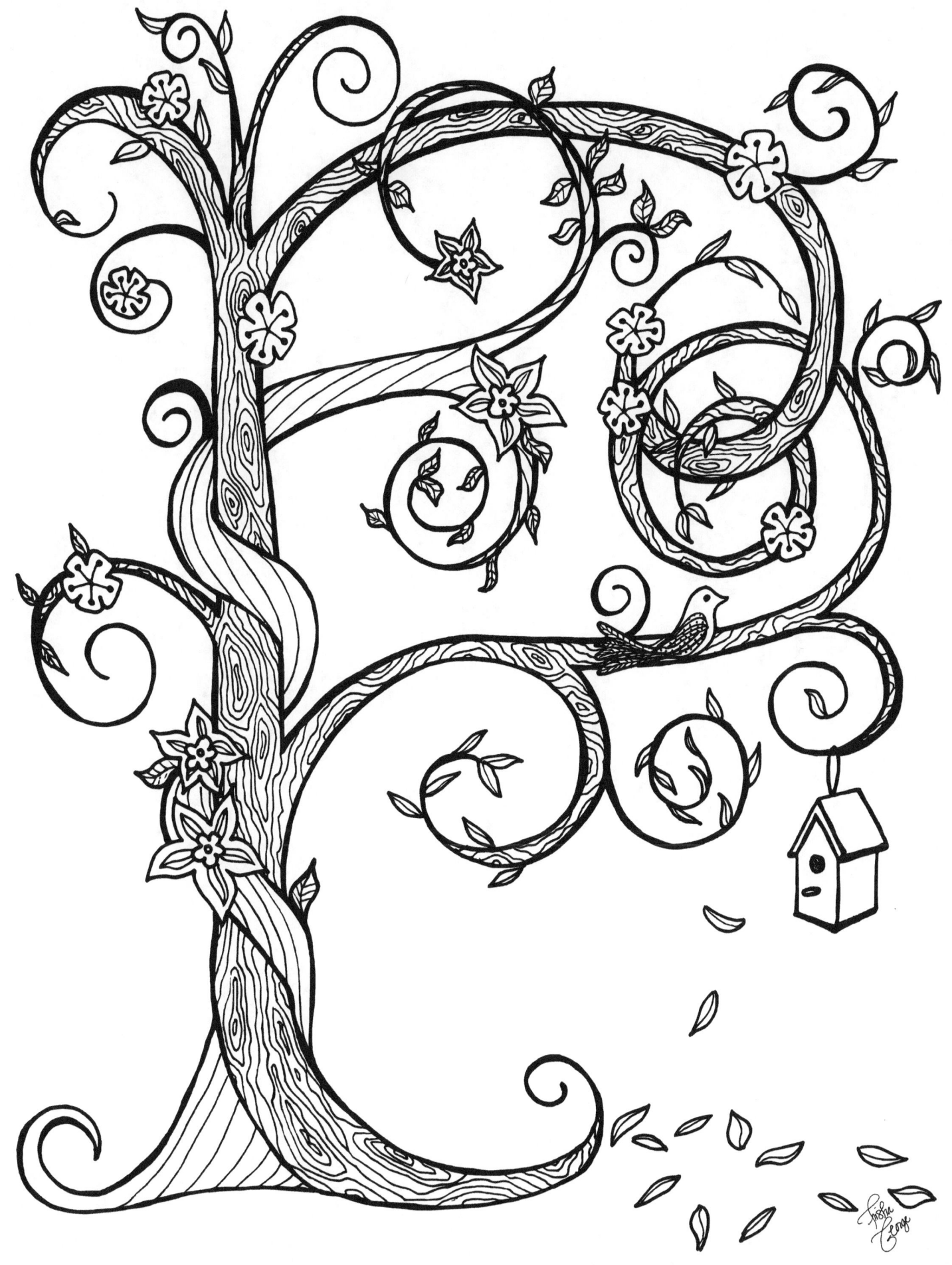

Colored By:

Date:

Techniques/Media Used:

Please use pencil to fill in information.

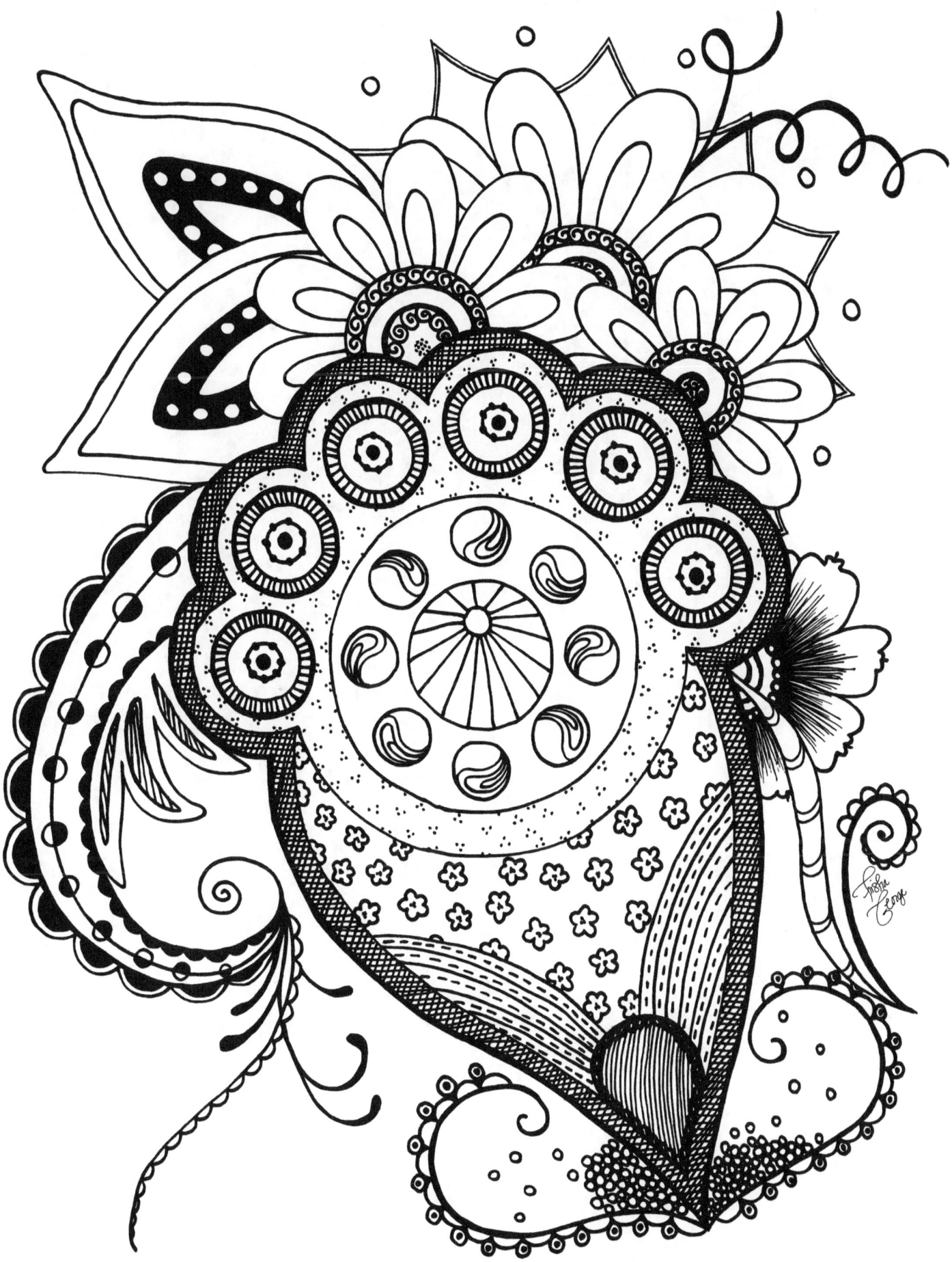

Colored By: _____

Date: _____

Techniques/Media Used: _____

_____

_____

Please use pencil to fill in information.

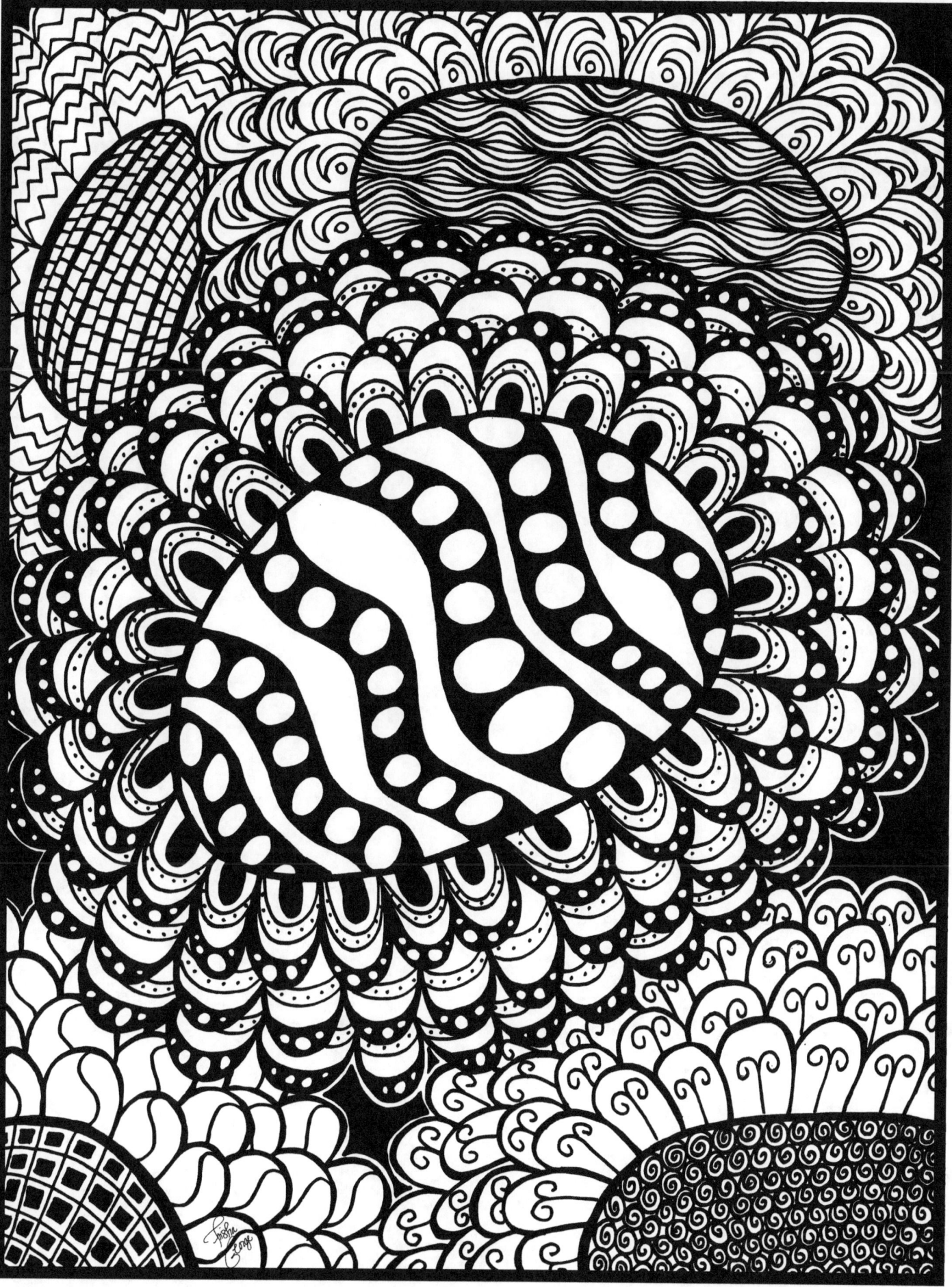

Colored By: _____

Date: _____

Techniques/Media Used: _____

_____

_____

Please use pencil to fill in information.

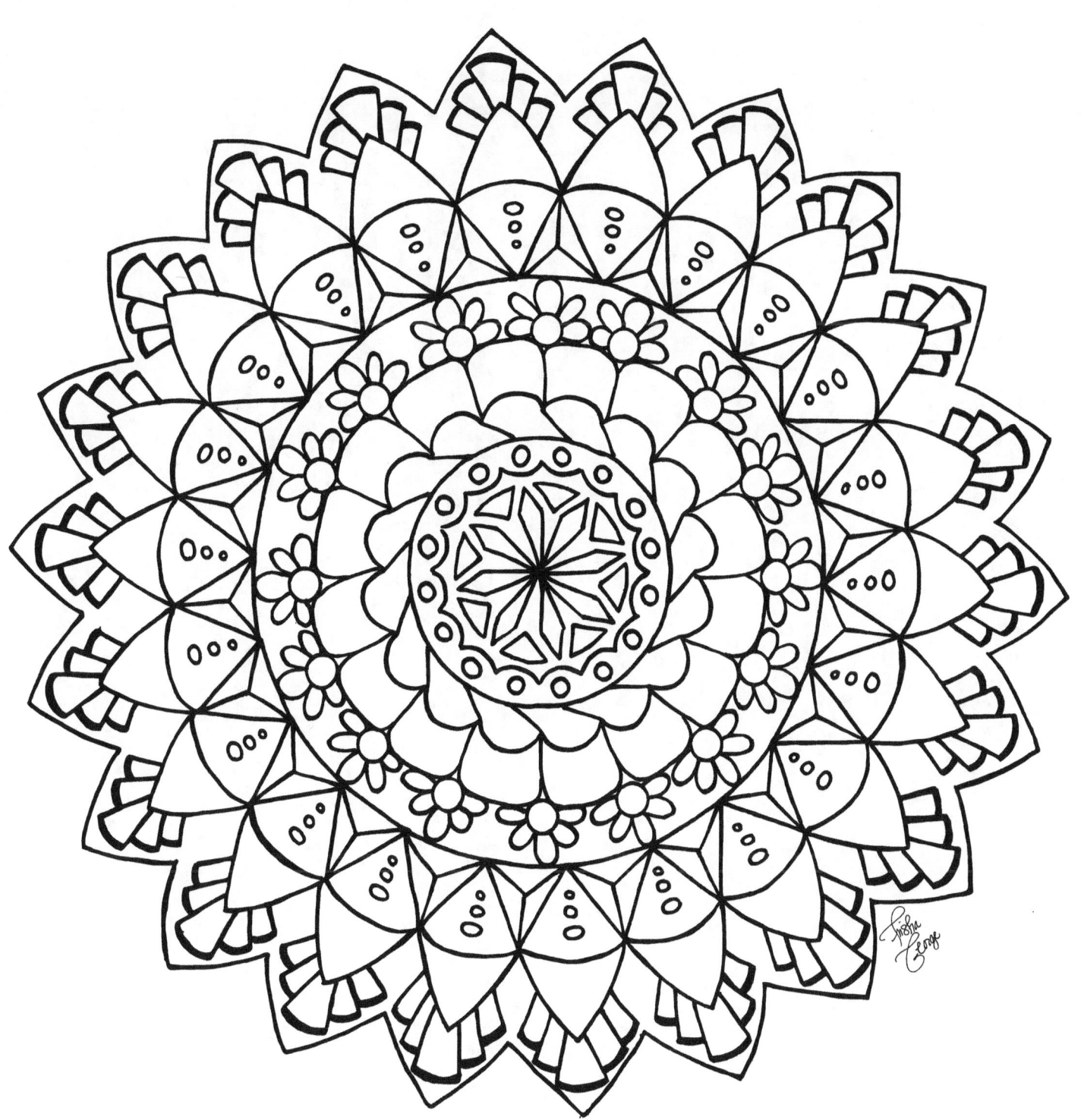

Colored By:_____

Date:_____

Techniques/Media Used:_____

_____

_____

Please use pencil to fill in information.

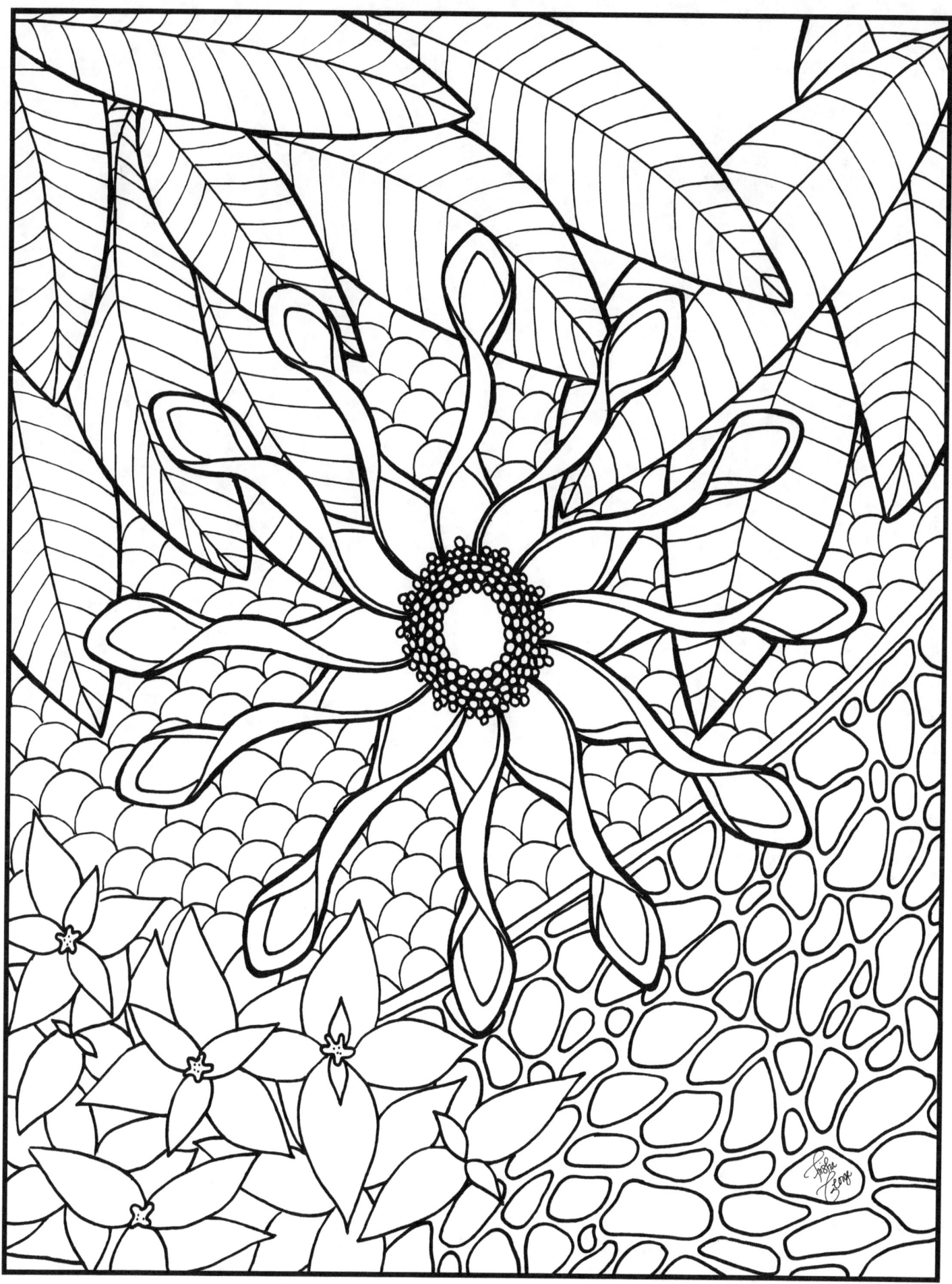

Colored By: _____

Date: _____

Techniques/Media Used: _____

_____

_____

Please use pencil to fill in information.

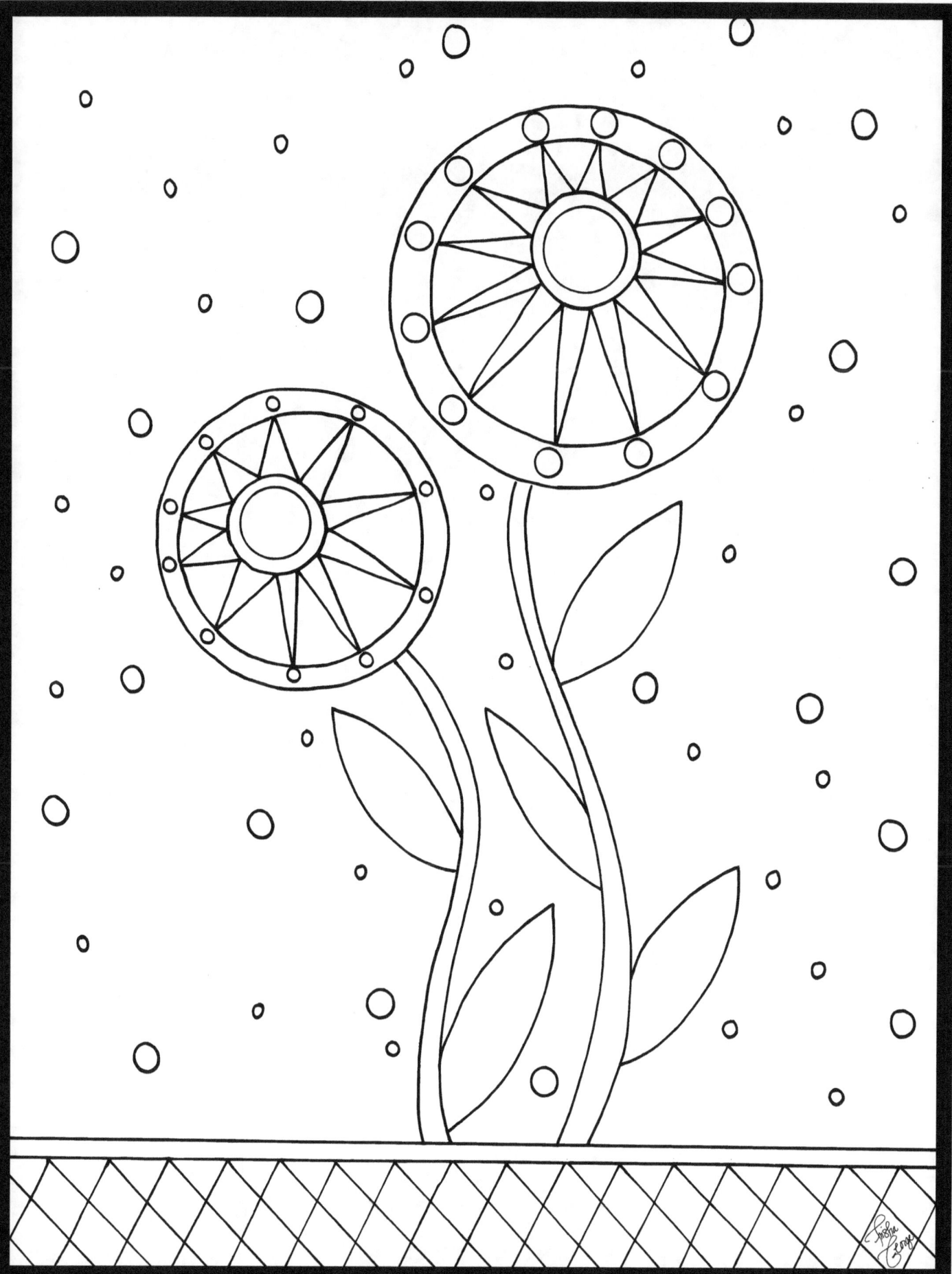

Colored By:_____

Date:_____

Techniques/Media Used:_____

_____

_____

_____

Please use pencil to fill in information.

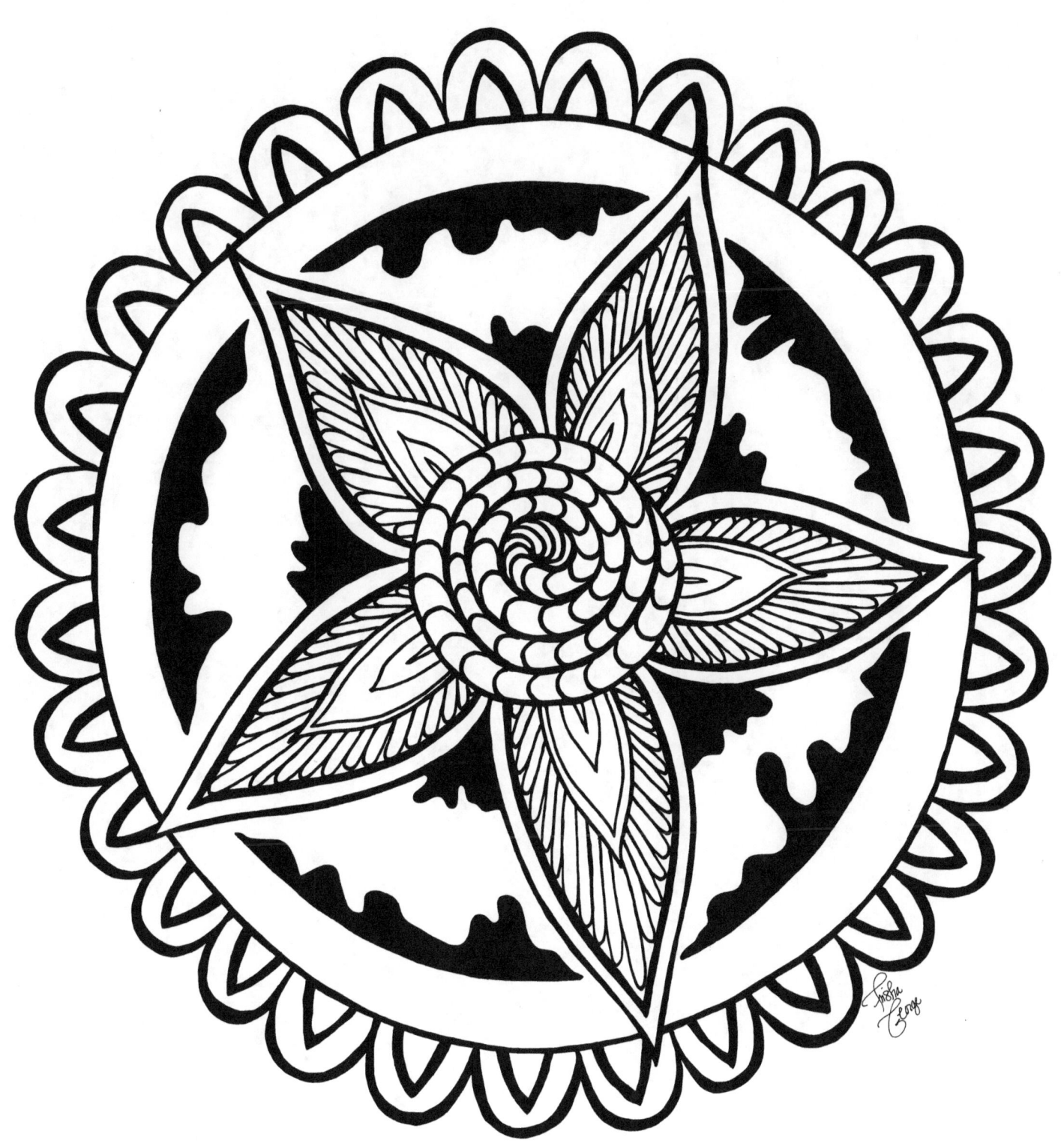

Colored By: _____

Date: _____

Techniques/Media Used: _____

_____

_____

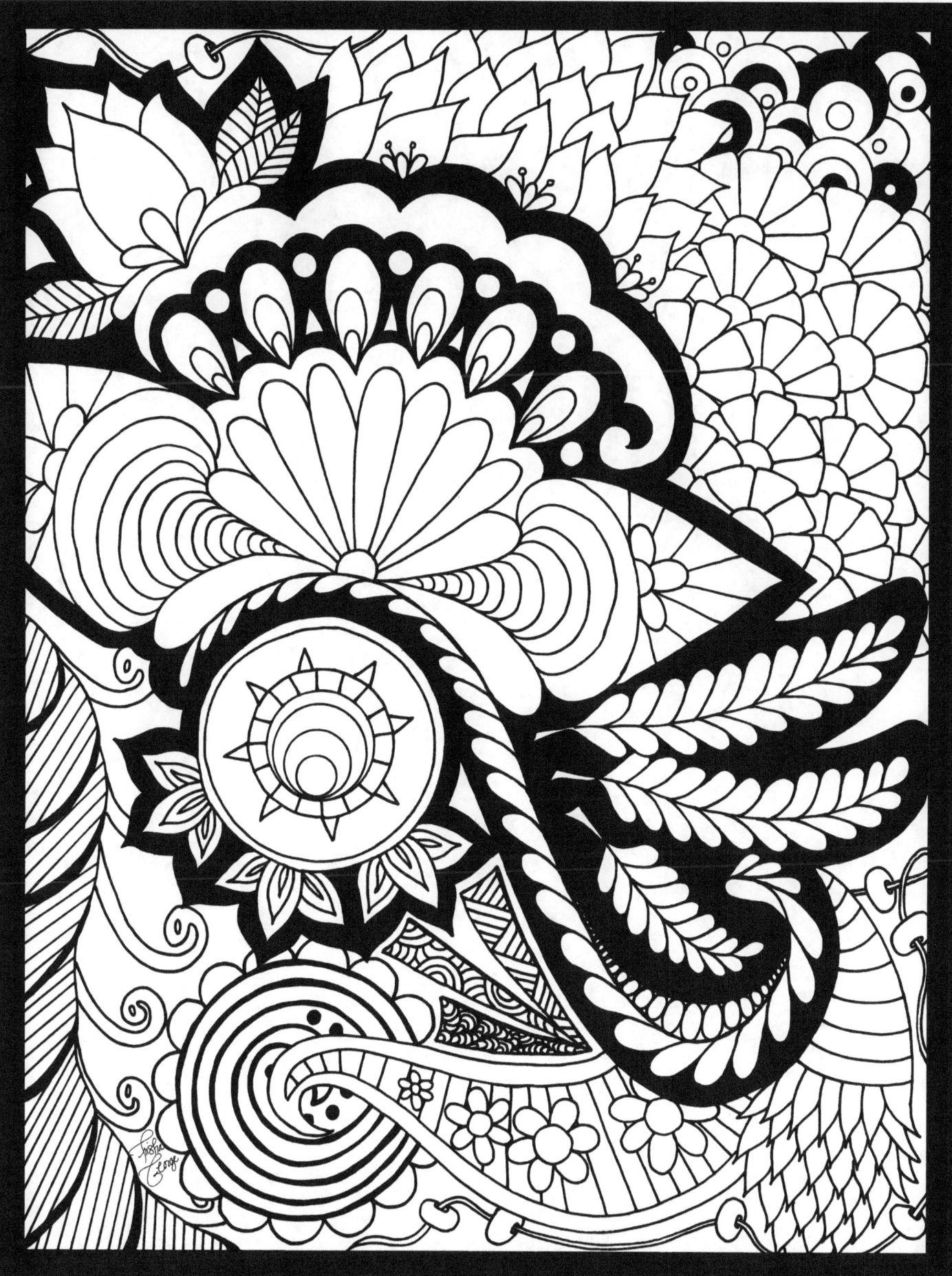

Colored By:_____

Date:_____

Techniques/Media Used:_____

_____

_____

Please use pencil to fill in information.

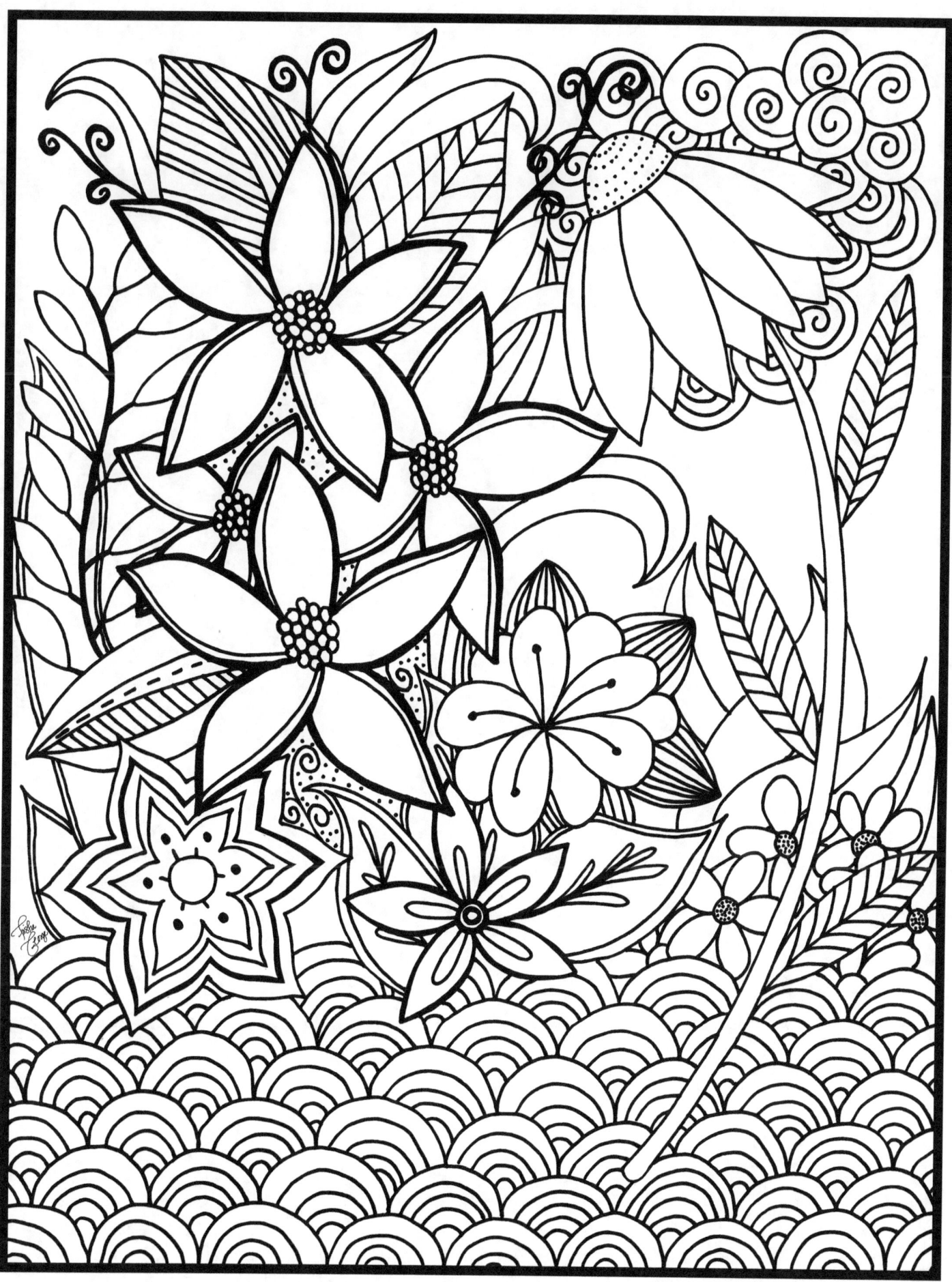

Colored By:_____

Date:_____

Techniques/Media Used:_____

_____

_____

Please use pencil to fill in information.

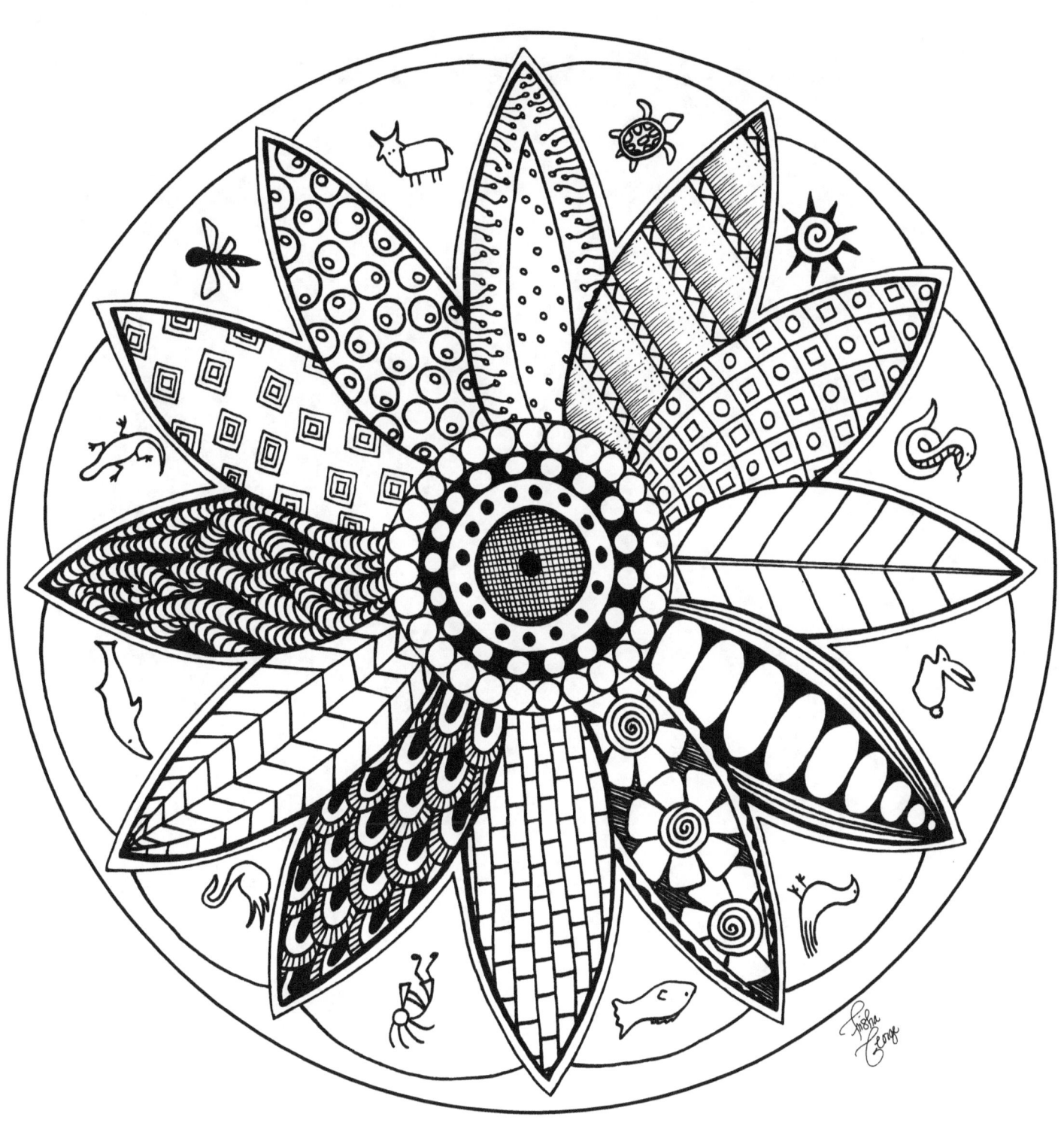

Colored By: _____

Date: _____

Techniques/Media Used: _____

_____

_____

Please use pencil to fill in information.

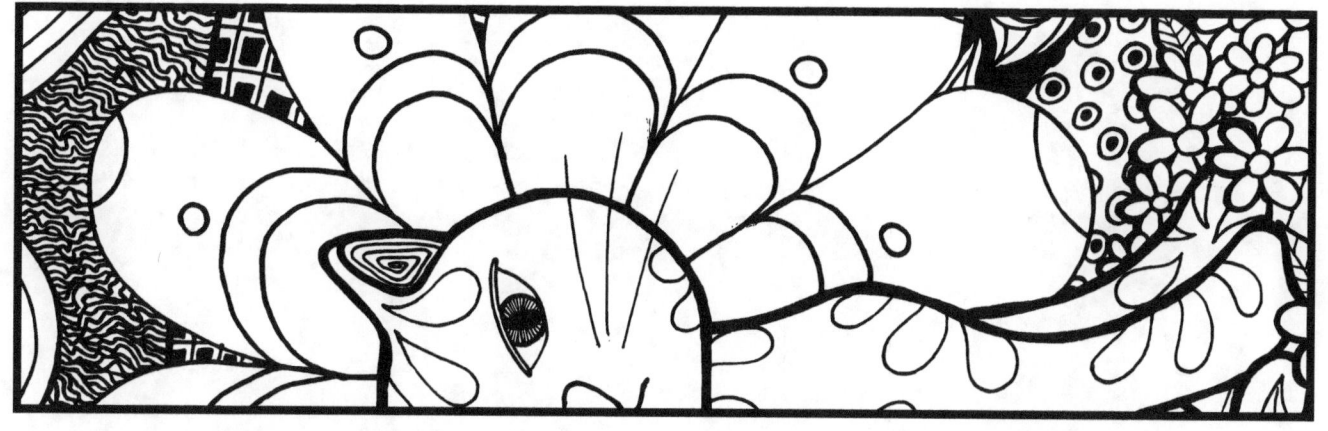

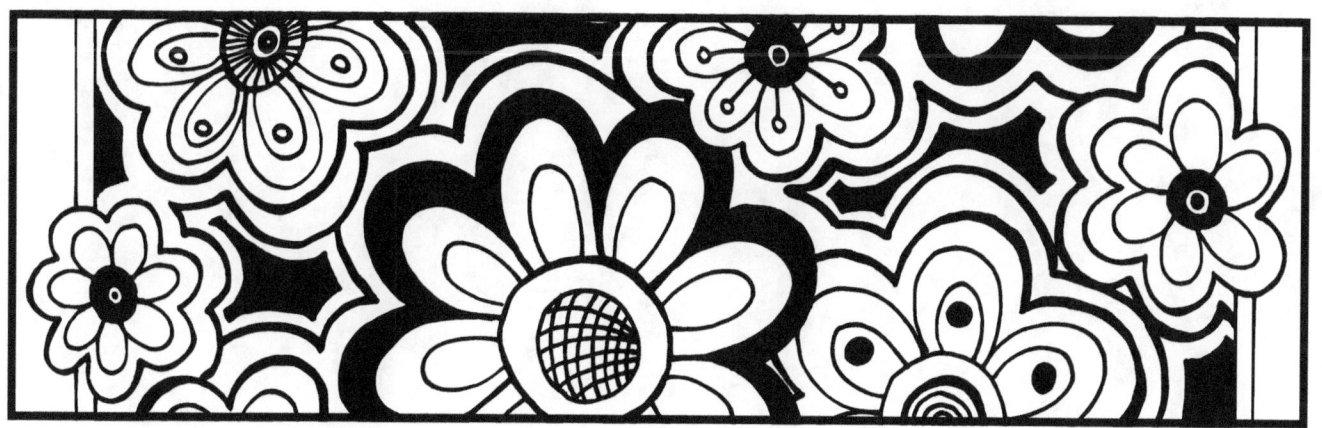

BOOKMARKS

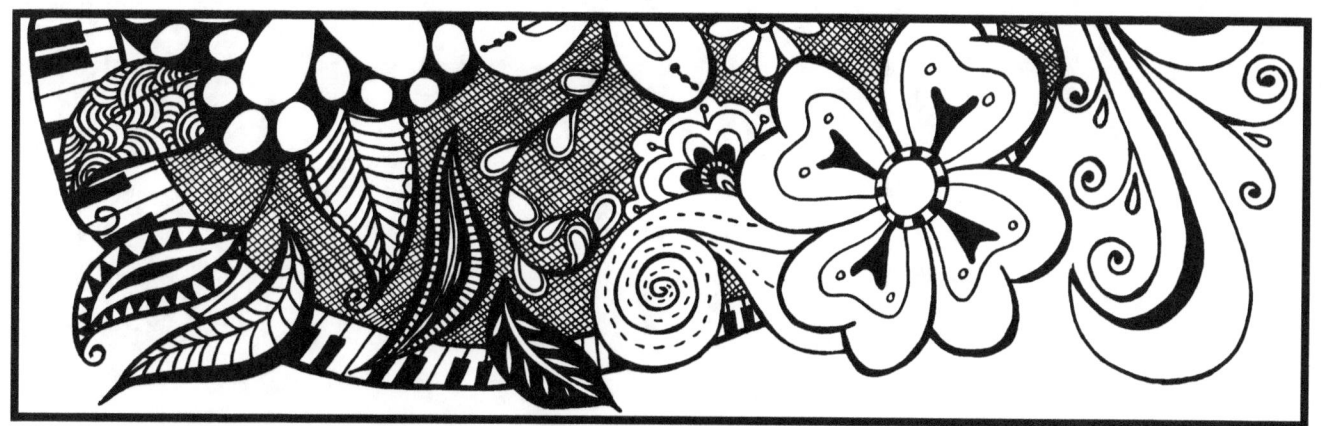

OTHER BOOKS BY THIS ARTIST

Creative Art Mandalas
Relaxing and Stress-Free Coloring

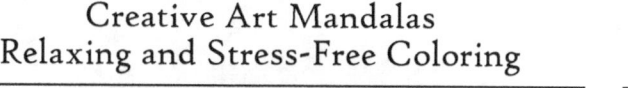

Geometric Pocket Mandalas
Mini Mandalas for On the Go

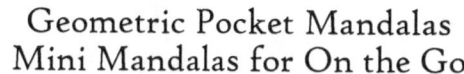

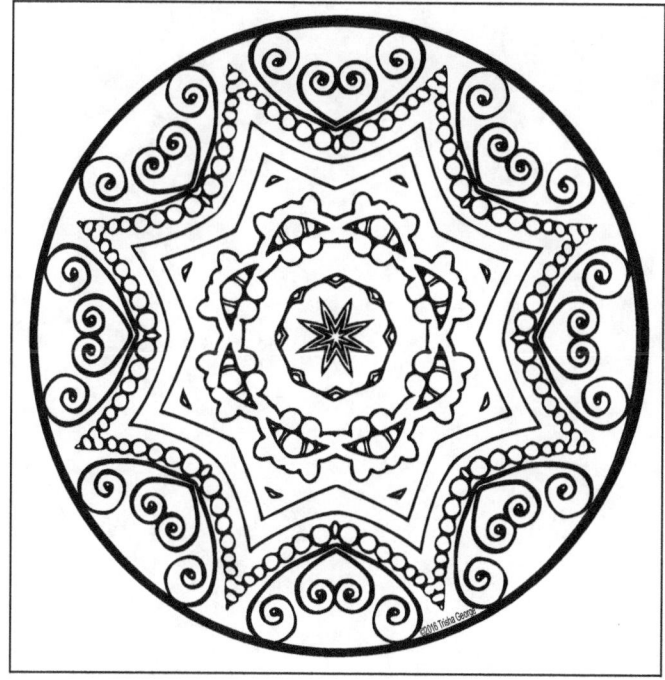

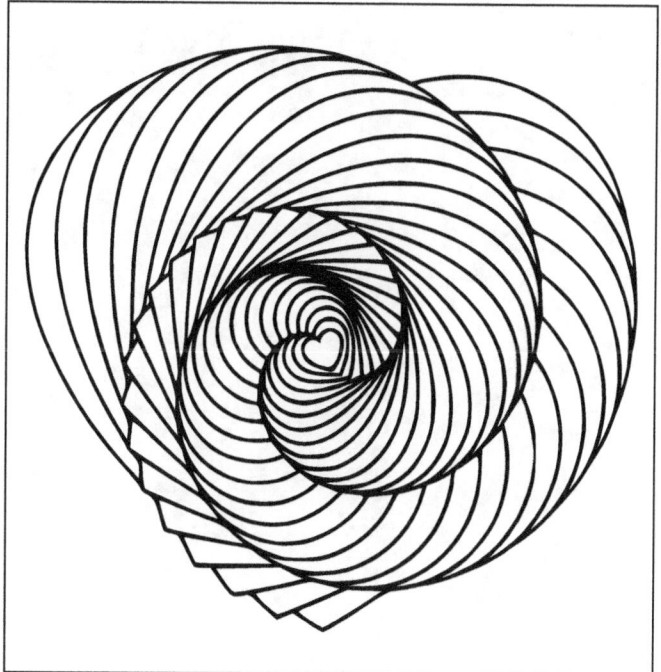

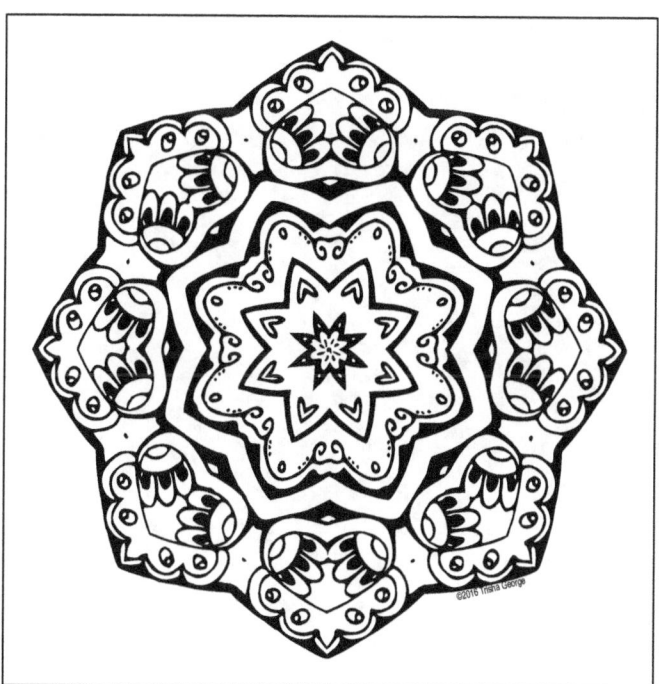

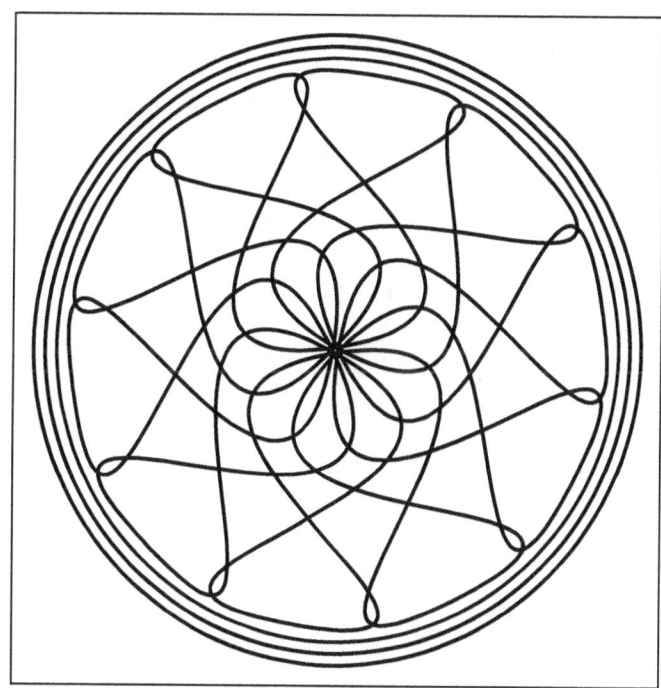

If you loved coloring this book, I would love it if you would leave positive feedback on Amazon. Good reviews help me sell more books which in turn helps me to produce even more fun and exciting coloring books for you!

Check out my website for new and upcoming books, coloring tips, and fun freebies!

www.TrishaGeorge.com

Dear Colorist,

The author gives you, the purchaser of this coloring book, permission to photocopy the pages in this book only for personal use. If you would like to use multiple images from this book for sharing, coloring parties, or any type of commercial use; please contact the author through her web page for a commercial license or party kit. Copying to distribute or for commercial use without prior permission from the copyright holder is in violation of U.S. Copyright law and is prohibited.

The three blotter pages included were created to cut out and place behind your coloring pages when using markers or other coloring media that might bleed through to the next coloring page. Usually one or two blotter pages is enough, though some very wet media may need multiple pages or card stock to prevent color bleed.

We hope that you will enjoy coloring this book and will follow the artist's web and social media pages. We also hope to see you post your completed pages to social media. Please give attribution to the artist. You may use the hashtag #TrishaGeorgeArt so we can find your colored images online. You can follow Trisha George at:

www.TrishaGeorge.com
Facebook: www.facebook.com/TrishaGeorgeArt
Instagram: TrishaGeorgeArt
Twitter: @TrishaGeorgeArt

Trisha George also has a facebook coloring group called Creative Art Coloring:

https://www.facebook.com/groups/CreativeArtColoring/

COME JOIN US!!

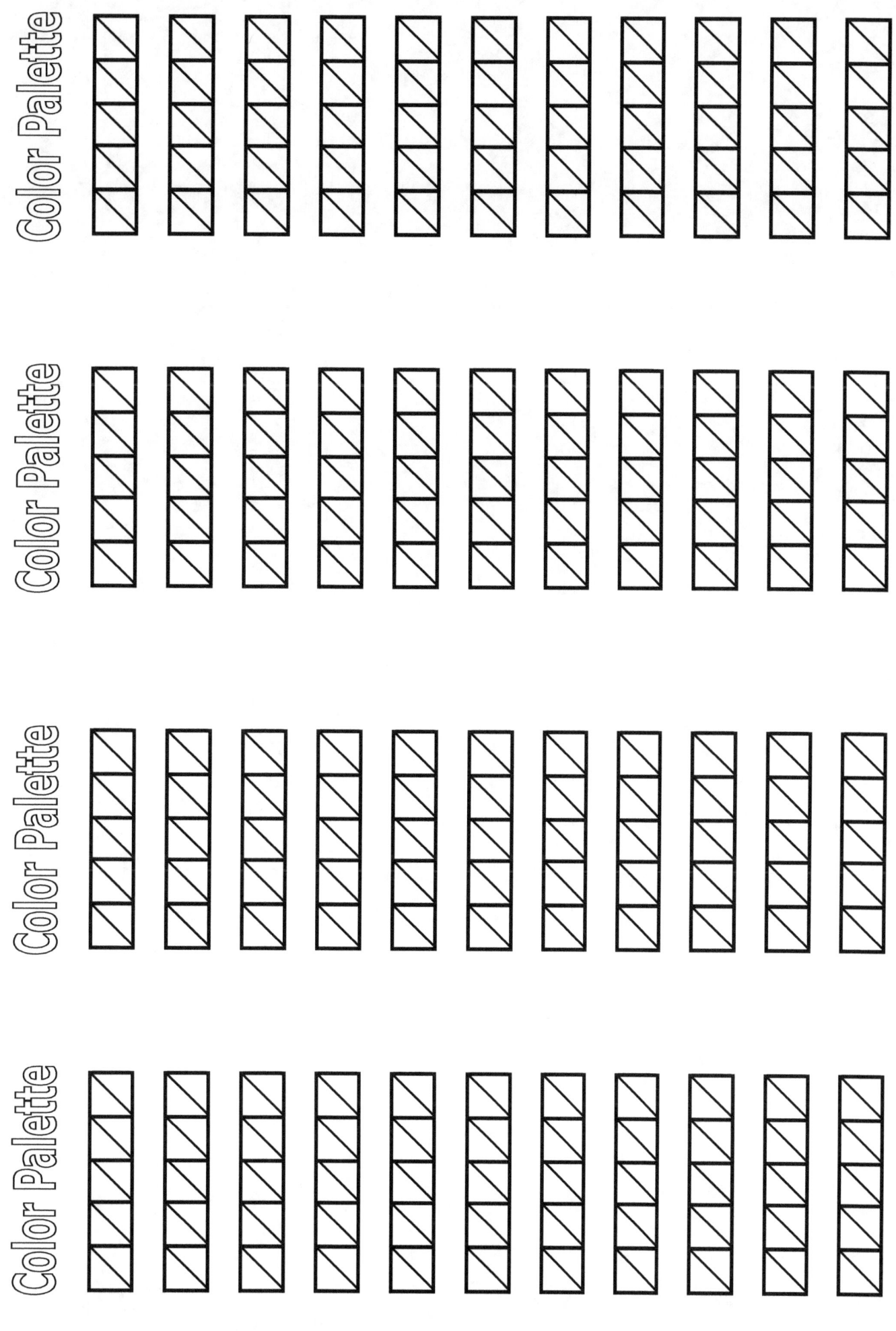

Color Palette

Color Palette

Color Palette

Color Palette

THE FRONT OF THIS PAGE CAN BE USED AS A BOOKMARK

* Carefully cut out the page with a craft knife *
* Fold it in half down the center of the four columns *
* Fold it in half again down the center of the remaining two columns *
* Use it to test your colors or for your chosen color palette *
* Use the spaces in between to write any notes or color names *

You will then have a folded bookmark showing all of your color choices
right with you while you are working on a coloring page. Remember to keep
a blotter page underneath this page if you leave it open to fill it in (if you are
using markers or gel pens) as they will often bleed through to the page behind it.

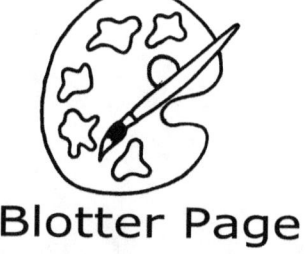

Blotter Page

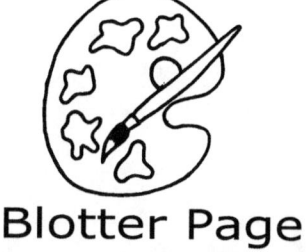

Blotter Page

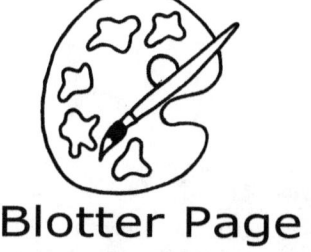

Blotter Page

www.ingramcontent.com/pod-product-compliance
Lightning Source LLC
Chambersburg PA
CBHW080540190526
45169CB00007B/2568